4/96

HOW TO LEARN A FOREIGN LANGUAGE

HOW TO LEARN A FOREIGN LANGUAGE

BY ARTHUR H. CHARLES, JR.

A SPEAK OUT, WRITE ON! BOOK
Franklin Watts
New York/Chicago/London/Toronto/Sydney

Library of Congress Cataloging-in-Publication Data

Charles, Arthur Howard.
How to learn a foreign language / by Arthur H. Charles, Jr.
p.   cm. — (A Speak out, write on! book)
Includes bibliographical references and index.
ISBN 0-531-11098-2
1. Language and languages—Study and teaching—Juvenile
literature.   [1. Language and languages—Study and teaching.]
I. Title.   II. Series.
P53.c427   1994
418'.007—dc20   93-29573
                                                                 CIP   AC

CONTENTS

ONE

WHY LEARN A FOREIGN LANGUAGE

So you want to learn a foreign language, or maybe you're not sure if you want to but part of your graduation requirement includes two or three years of foreign language study and you are not quite sure what lies in store for you. Or maybe you are in your first, second, or third year of studying a foreign language, are struggling with it, and wonder if you'll ever succeed or whether *fluency* is worth the struggle. Or maybe you know someone who can speak another language and you've been envious of that ability. Whatever your reasons for picking up this book may be, I'm glad that you did and I'll try my best to help your study of a foreign language come a little more easily.

REASONS FOR LEARNING A FOREIGN LANGUAGE

Maybe you already know some reasons why it is important to be able to communicate in more than one language. There is a time-honored saying that holds that "you are as many people as languages you speak." What this means is that a person who speaks three languages is as useful as three people who speak only one language each. Maybe even more so. Can you understand why?

Many Europeans speak three or four languages and therefore are able to communicate in at least one language with most people they meet. I remember a visit to a travel bureau in Lugano, Switzerland, to speak with my agent, a young Swiss man. We started speaking in Italian about my airline ticket, then he dialed a number in Zurich and explained about my problem in German, switched back to English with me while he was on hold, answered another client who asked him a question in French, and then went back into German when the airline representative came back on the phone. I marveled at how easily he was able to think and communicate in four languages without missing a beat!

If you speak only one language, even if it is a very popular language like English (spoken by more than 443 million people throughout the world), you are limited to speaking with those people who know your language. This means that you are missing out on communicating with hundreds of millions of people who do not know your language and you will not be able to learn more from them about their culture.

The world is getting smaller and smaller. You will have many more opportunities for travel and meeting non-Americans than your parents ever had. In 1992 Europe formed one large economic union, and American companies must respond to this monumental change. Therefore a great need exists in the business community for people who can speak more than just one language. If your portfolio of skills includes the ability to communicate in another language you will be a more attractive job applicant than another candidate with similar skills but no knowledge of another tongue.

Fine, so we have listed several reasons for learning a foreign language, but you may be wondering just what this task involves. If learning a foreign language is so important, does it have to be a struggle? And what does it take to really *know* another language, to be comfortably fluent in it?

"FOREIGN LANGUAGES"

First of all, let's look at the term "foreign language." What is language? In the next chapter we will look at what constitutes a language, what its various components consist of, and how these components combine to express meaning.

What does the term "foreign language" mean? We see that "foreign languages" are a part of our high school and university curricula. Three of the major foreign languages taught in American high schools are French, Spanish, and German. A language may be foreign to you because you do not use it every day. But there are 341 million people who use Spanish every day, some of them in various parts of the United States. There are 121 million people who use French on a daily basis; about 6 million of them reside in the Canadian province of Québec. Another 118 million people use German every day; the fact that they share the same language was one of the natural reasons why East and West Germans sought to form a single governmental unit.

Russian is spoken by more than 293 million people; while the major language(s) of the Indian subcontinent, Hindi/Urdu, have more than 442 million speakers. More than one-quarter of the earth's population speaks one form or other of Chinese; the major Chinese dialect, Mandarin, is spoken by 864 million people, almost twice the number who speak English. There are 197 million people who consider Arabic their native tongue. If you learn Japanese you will be speaking the native language of 125 million people. This is just to cite a few of the hundreds of languages spoken on our planet. [All figures taken from *The World Almanac and Book of Facts*.]

Hopefully, the language you are studying will not remain so "foreign" to you for very long. So instead of foreign language, let's refer to it as the *target language,* since mastery of that other language is your goal.

Latin, while not a living language, is the parent language for Italian, French, Spanish, Rumanian, Portuguese and Romansch, and is taught in many high schools in the United States and Europe. These languages are called *"Romance languages"* because they all belong to the same linguistic family, all descended from the parent language of Latin, which was spread by the conquering Roman armies two thousand years ago. These languages share many vocabulary items that are similar in form (called *"cognates"*). This often makes it easier for a speaker of one of the Romance languages to understand a speaker of another Romance language. For example, compare the following list of vocabulary items:

Latin	French	Spanish	Italian	(English)
unus	un	uno	uno	(one)
porta	porte	puerta	porta	(door)
filius	fils	hijo	figlio	(son)
totus	tout	todo	tutto	(all)
liber	livre	libro	libro	(book)
habere	avoir	haber	avere	(to have)

One of the reasons why a number of American schools continue to offer Latin as part of their curriculum is that many vocabulary items in English have Latin roots. Modern English is not derived from Latin, but from Anglo-Saxon. However, after the Norman conquest of 1066 a number of Latin vocabulary items (most having to do with government, church, military, literature, and culture) that were used by the French-speaking conquerors were absorbed into the language that would eventually become English. Thus we have *liberate, lib-*

eral from Latin **liber**, "free"; *populate, population* from Latin **populus**, "people"; *militia, military* from Latin **miles**, "soldier"; *paternal, paternity* from Latin **pater**, "father".

TASK OR ADVENTURE?

Don't be daunted by the task that lies before you. Think of it as an adventure that will open many doors when you have mastered this skill. In many ways you can think of learning another language like learning to ride a bike. Remember how excited, but scared, you were with the idea of learning to ride a bike? But once you had mastered this skill, you suddenly became able to travel more quickly and go greater distances. The skill you mastered came at the expense of a few bruises, to your body and pride. Well, learning a foreign language is a bit the same. You'll stumble, make a few mistakes (maybe even a couple of embarrassing ones), but when you have finally mastered another language you will feel a sense of pride in your accomplishment and your new skill will be a passport to even greater adventures.

Don't worry whether or not you have an "aptitude" for learning a foreign language. Ordinary people of average intelligence manage to speak and understand two, three, or four languages because it is part of their experience to have frequent contact with speakers of other languages. (For example, the travel agent in Lugano or the German truck driver who hauls cargo across half a dozen countries.) So, why can't it be the same for you? More important than your "aptitude" for foreign languages will be your *commitment* in determining your success in learning another language.

The purpose of this book is to give you an idea of what is involved in mastering another language. It contains some explanations about language in general and some languages in particular.

HINTS AND SUGGESTIONS

This book is aimed primarily at students who are learning a foreign language in a class situation. As we go along in this book you will receive a few hints or suggestions to help you discover ways to learn a language skill. What follows is a list of dos and don'ts to prepare you for learning a foreign language.

When I asked a fellow language teacher for suggestions to give students in how to learn a foreign language, he gave me his rule #1: *Attend class.* (He told me that he believes in basics.) Humor aside, it is difficult enough to try to master a language by spending only 45 minutes a day, 5 days a week, 180 days (maximum) a year. Plus, your teacher's attention is divided between you and the dozen to two dozen other students in the class. So you can maximize your learning potential by never missing class and by paying careful attention to what is presented in class.

Keep a separate notebook or loose-leaf binder for your language class. That way, you'll have an easy reference to material you have learned. Take profuse notes in class; be especially sure to write down everything that your teacher writes on the board. Remember that if he/she thinks it's important enough to write on the board he/she probably expects you to learn it. Here's another suggestion for taking notes. Don't worry about taking neat notes. In fact, it's better to take lots of sloppy notes than too few that do not adequately cover the material your teacher is presenting. Try taking your notes on a legal pad, then recopying the notes in the evening, when you are studying. This is a great way to review and reinforce what you have covered that day in class.

Do your homework. Consider homework an opportunity to review material you have already covered in class and to prepare for what is to come. You can't discuss on the next day a selection you forgot to read the night before.

Get to know your teacher. Teaching/learning is a cooperative process. The more you are "in sync" with your teacher's interests, the more you share his or her enthusiasm for the language, the more you will learn because your teacher will make sure that you learn.

Don't make your goal to learn about the language; *learn to use it!* You can learn all you want about a bicycle, its parts, and the physics involved with riding a bike, but until you get up on it and start pedaling you will never be able to actually ride a bike.

Don't be afraid to make mistakes. Even native speakers of a foreign language occasionally make mistakes. (If you think about it, you probably make plenty of mistakes in English. If you're not sure, check with your English teacher!) Remember how many times you fell trying to ride that bike. If you were too afraid to fall you never would have learned to ride the bike.

Don't try to translate into English or compare the foreign language with English. There is no one "correct" way of expressing an idea. In fact, each language has a different way of explaining the world. (More on that later.)

Don't wait! The sooner you get started, the better. Younger children may have a better "ear" for the sounds and pronunciation of a foreign language, but high school students have better analytical skills.

As much as possible *familiarize yourself with the country* or countries where the language you are studying is spoken. Locate the country(ies) on a map, learn about the topography (i.e., mountains, rivers, etc.), major cities, bordering countries, population size. Read a book or travel guide on the customs and culture of the people(s) who speak the language. That way you will be well versed in terms of the people, country, customs, and culture that speakers of "your" new language talk about.

Good luck. **Bonne chance. Viel Glück. Buona fortuna. Buena suerte.**

THE COMPONENTS OF LANGUAGE

The purpose of this chapter is to provide an overview of how language in general and all languages in particular operate. It will present the components and features of language and will discuss how some features may be the same in English and the target language, while other linguistic features may be different in the two languages. As you might deduce, those features your target language shares with English will be easier to learn than those features that are different in the two languages.

Each and every language spoken on this planet is a *system*, made up of subsystems, which in turn are made up of different components. As with any system, there are specific rules that govern the ways in which the subsystems of the language operate. Understanding more about how the subsystems of English operate and becoming aware of how the subsystems of the target language operate will enable you to take the first steps in mastering the other language.

LANGUAGE SUBSYSTEMS

The first subsystem of any language is its *phonology*, or sound system. Every utterance, from the shortest phrase to the longest speech ever delivered, can basically be reduced to the individual sounds or phonemes that make it up. Sounds in any language occur one after the other and can occur only in certain combinations. Before languages were ever written down, mankind had been speaking for tens of thousands of years. We can imagine that when people first started using language they began by experimenting with sounds in different combinations and relating those combinations of sounds to things or events in their experience. (At the sight of three charging woolly mammoths, Oog turned to Ugg and yelled "Zagg, zagg, zagg!") They spoke and listened to one another long before inventing symbols to represent their thoughts and before writing down these symbols. Prehistoric (the word means "before written records") men and women used speech to communicate about various aspects of daily living: the weather, how the food tasted, where the best hunting spot was for woolly mammoths.

In considering the system of sounds of a language, however, you must not confuse sounds with the letters that are the written symbols for those sounds. Bear in mind that any piece of writing from a roadside sign to the contents of a note to a friend, to a play by Shakespeare is a visual representation of what is originally and essentially an oral activity; language is first and foremost oral. The written word cannot capture all the nuances of sound, the pitch, the intonation of speech. (Consider that three actors reading the same line of a play may give three entirely different oral interpretations of the same written material.)

In English, and some other languages, there is not always a close correspondence between sounds and their written symbols, letters. For example, English contains forty-three sounds, as opposed to its twenty-six letters. You may even have heard that the word *fish* can be spelled GHOTI in English. That is, if we take the sound represented by *gh* in *enough*, plus the sound of *o* in *women*, followed by the sound of *ti* in *action* we will arrive at a word sounding like *fish*. (Try to explain that one to the officials of a spelling bee!)

Languages do not all share the same number of sounds. Another way of saying this is that, given the pool of all the possible sounds employed by all the languages of the world, no single language makes use of all of these sounds; each language uses only a limited number of all possible language sounds. Sounds that occur in one language may or may not occur in a second language. Two languages that belong to the same larger linguistic family will tend to share more sounds and sound features than two languages from different linguistic families. Thus, all the sounds of English may not be found in another language you are studying; and the target language may contain some sounds that do not occur in English. French has nine vowels, four of which are nasal vowels that don't occur in English, German, or Japanese. This is important to keep in mind, and we will discuss it further in the chapter dealing with listening and speaking.

Individual sounds can be grouped into larger units of sound known as *syllables*, which are essentially breath groups of sounds separated from one another by brief pauses. Different languages have different rules for how sounds may combine with one another to form syllables, which sounds can occur in juxtaposition (i.e., next to one another), and the maximum and minimum number of sounds that may occur in a syllable. For example, the combination of the three consonants **/str/** is quite common in English (e.g., **strike, stretch, restrain**) but could never occur in a large number of languages. The combination of the two consonants **/sk/** can occur in word initial position in English (e.g., **school, ski, scare**), but it must always be preceded by a vowel in Spanish (e.g., **escuela, escribir**).

In English, French, Spanish, and German there are as many syllables in an utterance as there are *pronounced vowels.* In English a syllable can contain from one to seven sounds (e.g., **strengths/strɛnθs/** and **scrunched/skrənčt/**, because the syllable nucleus, the vowel, can be preceded and followed by as many as three consonants). In French and Italian the maximum number of sounds in a syllable is fewer. Compare, for example, the syllable *structure* of English, in which syllables tend to end in consonants, with Romance languages, in which syllables tend to end in vowels. For example,

> (English) **gen-er-al; res-taur-ant; con-tin-ent**
> (French) **gé-né-ral; re-stau-rant; con-ti-nent**
> (in French **ant/on/ent** are nasal vowels)
> (Italian) **ge-ne-ra-le; ri-sto-ran-te; con-ti-nen-te**

In Japanese the typical syllable structure is either a vowel or a consonant followed by a vowel. In Hindi most syllables are made up of a consonant followed by a vowel, and almost all consonants occur singly, that is, each consonant is separated from the next by a vowel. (In written Hindi, consonants may be juxtaposed, but when read aloud a vowel sound /ə/ is pronounced between these consonants.)

In summary, languages may differ as to the sounds they employ and as to how these sounds occur in relation to one another.

The second subsystem of language is its *morphology,* the manner in which words are constructed. Look at the following pairs of words:

CAT CATS
ASK ASKED
FIT UNFIT

Each of the above is a word. However, you can also recognize that the difference between **CAT** and **CATS** is the *suffix* **-S**, which, although it is not a word, carries a meaning (that of "plural" or "more than one"). The difference between **ASK** and **ASKED** is the suffix **-ED**, which carries the meaning of "past tense" or "completed action." The difference between **FIT** and **UNFIT** is the *prefix* **UN-**, which carries the meaning of "not." These prefixes or suffixes are not words in themselves but are *units of meaning* or *morphemes.* Thus the word **CAT** contains one unit of meaning; the word **CATS** has two. **ASK** contains a single morpheme; **ASKED** contains two. (How many morphemes are contained in the words *neighborhood, actors, friends, unfriendly, codified*?)

There is no relationship between the number of sounds and the number of morphemes in a word or utterance. For example, in English, **UNDERSTAND** contains ten *phonemes* but is made up of a single morpheme, whereas **CATS** is made up of four phonemes and contains two morphemes.

However, not every occurrence of a sound or group of sounds is a morpheme. For example the **UN-** of **UNFIT** is a morpheme because it carries a meaning; the **UN-** of **UNDER** or **FUN** has no meaning in itself and is not a morpheme.

The morphology of a language deals with the rules by which the language combines units of meaning (morphemes) into words. According to systems of morphology or the ways in which words are constructed, there are different types of languages. Latin is an *inflective* language. In inflective languages the stem carries the meaning of the word, but the stem never occurs alone; it always occurs with an ending that indicates its function. For example, take a look at the following Latin sentence,

Agricola puellam videt.
(The farmer sees the girl.)

The stem **agricol-** carries the meaning of "farmer," while the ending tells us that the word serves as the subject of the sentence. Likewise, **puell-** carries the meaning of "girl," while **-am** indicates that this word is the direct object of the verb **videt**. Because the suffixes carry grammatical meaning, word order is not important in Latin and the same meaning could also be conveyed by

Puellam agricola videt.
Videt agricola puellam.
Agricola videt puellam.

Similarly, in the sentence

Puellae agricolam vident.
(The girls see the farmer.)

puell- still carries the meaning of "girl," while the ending **-ae** indicates a "plural, subject"; **agricol-** carries the meaning of "farmer," while **-am** indicates "singular, object of the verb." You can see from these two sentences how important the role of the suffixes is in Latin.

Now let's look at the English translation for the above two Latin sentences:

The farmer sees the girl.
The girls see the farmer.

In English the stem words, *girl, farmer,* and *see* can stand alone, while the suffix **-s** added to **girl** indicates "plural" and added to **see** conveys the idea of "third-person singular subject, present tense." We can also see that in a language such as English *word order* plays a much more important role than in Latin. Compare the difference between

The girl sees the farmer.
The farmer sees the girl.

There is also a relationship between the morphology and the phonology of a language in that each morpheme is made up of one or more units of sound or phonemes. For example, in English the "plural" morpheme has several different sound (or phonological) shapes. Compare, for example, the sound of **-S** in the following plural words: **CATS, DOGS, HORSES**. How would you describe the plural morpheme for **OXEN** or **GEESE**?

We can compare how different languages deal with the plural morpheme:

the dog	**the dogs**	(English)
le chien	**les chiens**	(French)
el perro	**los perros**	(Spanish)
der Hund	**die Hunde**	(German)

Note that in English the noun changes its form by adding a plural suffix, but the article remains unchanged in form, while in French, German, and Spanish both the definite article and the noun change their form. However, in French the plural suffix **/-s/** remains silent, so the change in the sound or phonemic composition of the *definite article* signals that the accompanying noun is plural.

The third major subsystem of language is its *syntax*, or the rules for combining words into larger groups of meaning, phrases and sentences.

Each language has its own set of rules by which words combine into phrases, phrases combine into clauses, and clauses combine into sentences. For example, a noun phrase in English would follow this pattern:

NP →	Det	+	Adj	+	Adj	+	N
	the		tall		French		boy
	two		small				books
	a		red		Italian		bicycle

and in German:

NP →	Det	+	Adj	+	Adj	+	N
	das		grosse		englische		Fahrrad
	der		kleine		schwarze		Zug

(which is essentially the same pattern for a noun phrase in English); while in Italian the pattern would be

NP →	Det	+	Adj	+	N	+	Adj	+	Adj
	il		grande		ragazzo		francese		
	due		piccoli		libri				
	una				bicicletta		italiana		rossa

and in French:

NP →	Det	+	Adj	+	N	+	Adj	+	Adj
	le		grand		garçon		italien		
	deux		petits		livres				
	un				vélo		français		rouge

Note that in German and English the adjectives appear before the noun, while in Italian and French some adjectives appear before the noun and others occur after the noun. However, in all three languages noun phrases generally begin with *determiners*.

Another example of the difference in structure would be the position of pronouns in a sentence. Note the difference between the pattern in English:

Sent ⇸	Subj	+	Verb	+	Dir.Obj.Pn	+	Ind.Obj.
	I		sold		it		to Mary
	We		gave		them		to him

while in French, the structure would be:

Sent ⇸	Subj	+	Pn	+	Pn	+	Verb	+	Ind.Obj.
	Je		l'				ai vendu		à Marie
	Nous		les		lui		avons donnés		

In many languages there is an interrelationship between the subject and a verb that is reflected in the ending of the verb showing whether the subject is first, second, or third person, singular or plural. Some examples in Spanish and German:

yo hablo	ich spreche	(I speak)
tú hablas	du sprichst	(you speak)
nosotros hablamos	wir sprechen	(we speak)

SKILLS FOR LANGUAGE MASTERY

If you are going to become fluent in a foreign language then you have to master the following four *linguistic* skills:

	passive ↔ active	
(aural/oral)	LISTENING	SPEAKING
(written)	READING	WRITING
	(*decoding*)	(*encoding*)

It is not sufficient to concentrate on one or two of these skills if you truly wish to be fluent. You may hear someone say "I can understand it when they speak it, but I can't say a word!" That person is far from being fluent.

Usually in learning a foreign language you move from the passive skills (listening comprehension and reading) to the active skills (speaking and writing, respectively). That is to say, before you can speak the foreign language you begin by listening to your teacher or a speaker of the language as he/she uses it and you attempt to distinguish the sounds, the units of meaning, and the ideas in the stream of speech. The speech you hear becomes the trigger for your own speech, often in the form of answers to questions you are asked. Similarly, before you can write freely in a foreign language you usually read passages in the language and then answer written questions about its content.

Though interrelated, each of these skills has distinctive features that require particular attention if mastery is to be achieved.

Listening is a passive linguistic skill of decoding that involves being able to distinguish the differences in sounds and sound features uttered by a speaker that make for a difference in meaning; being able to recognize words and larger structures; and being able to recognize the components that combine to form ideas.

Speaking is the active linguistic skill that involves encoding the ideas you want to transmit into speech that can be understood by the listener because the speech follows rules for pronunciation as well as word, phrase, and sentence structure.

Reading is the passive linguistic skill that involves the ability to decode the meaningful units on a written page and to understand the general meaning of the individual words which are used together.

Writing is the active linguistic skill that involves the ability to transmit ideas by stringing together in a grammatically and orthographically correct manner the vocabulary items used to convey these ideas.

Mastery of a foreign language means being able to understand sentences and passages that you may hear or read for the first time as well as being able to produce in speech or writing original thoughts and sentences. Fluency in a foreign language means being able to *react creatively* in language to new situations you may encounter.

While learning a foreign language may involve focusing on a particular skill during part of a language class—e.g., practice on recognizing and producing a particular sound; reading a long passage for comprehension; practicing a dialogue for pronunciation; discussing a reading passage; writing a composition—it will soon become apparent to you that the four linguistic skills are interrelated. Indeed, true fluency in a foreign language requires mastery of all four skills, not just being able to understand it when it is spoken or reading a newspaper in the foreign language.

There is one other skill that is important for language mastery; knowing how to interpret and use the *body language* of the target culture. Body language includes such features as arm and hand gestures, facial expressions, tones, and stance that accompany oral speech. These features are used by both the speaker and listener. Aspects of body language will vary from culture to culture.

THREE

GRAMMAR, THE RULES OF LANGUAGE

The *grammar* of a language includes both its morphology and syntax; that is, a language's grammar is the set of rules for the formation of words, phrases, and sentences and their interrelationships. A firm grasp of a language's grammar is necessary for communicating clearly and effectively in the language.

Knowledge of the grammar rules is the cement that ties the four linguistic skills together. This knowledge enables you to decode the relationship between words in sentences you hear and read; it enables you to produce in speech and writing sentences that are understandable, that is, grammatically correct.

Learn all that you can about the grammar of English. There will be many terms used in describing the components and operations in English that will be similar to those used to describe other languages. For example, the parts of speech you study in English have their parallels in most other foreign languages that you are likely to study.

PARTS OF SPEECH

The term "parts of speech" refers to the categories into which words can be grouped according to the grammatical functions they play in larger structures. The designations for the major parts of speech are as follows:

Nouns are words used to name people, places, things, concepts. (English nouns would include: *brother, London, coffee, beauty.*)

Pronouns are words that take the place of nouns. (In English *I/me, you, he/him, she/her, it, we/us, they/them* are examples of pronouns.)

Verbs are words that indicate actions or states of being. (English verbs would include: *to write, to run, to remain, to become, to live.*)

Adjectives are words used to modify or describe nouns. (Some examples from English would be: *large, tiny, clear, red, happy.*)

Adverbs are words that modify or qualify verbs, adjectives or other adverbs (English adverbs would include: *well, quickly, frequently.*)

Prepositions are words used to introduce phrases. (English prepositions would include: *for, to, from, because of.*)

Conjunctions are words used to connect phrases, clauses, or sentences. (In English *and, or, because, since* would be examples of conjunctions.)

Determiners are words used to mark nouns. The most common determiners are:

definite article (*the* in English)
indefinite article (*a/an, some* in English)
demonstratives (*this, that, these, those* in English)
possessives (*my, your, his, her, its, our, their* in English)
numerals (*one, seven, two million* in English)

An awareness of how the various parts of speech are used in relation to one another (in other words, the grammar) allows us to classify the nonsense words of Lewis Carroll's "Jabberwocky":

'Twas brillig, and the slithy toves
Did gyre and gimble in the wabe
All mimsy were the borogroves. . . .

Though these nonsense words have no real meaning you could identify "toves," "wabe," and "borogroves" as nouns; "gyre" and "gimble" as *verbs*; "slithy" and "mimsy" as adjectives because of their position in relation to one another and because the other words give signals as to their grammatical function.

GRAMMATICAL CONCEPTS

There are also grammatical concepts relating to verbs and nouns in English that may be applied to the use of nouns and verbs in the foreign language you are studying. What is significant is that these distinctions may often be reflected in differences in form.

Nouns can be described as to *gender, number,* and *case.* Most languages distinguish nouns as being *masculine* or *feminine;* other languages, including Latin and German, have a third gender, *neuter.* As to number, nouns are generally either *singular* or *plural.* (Some languages, such as Arabic, use the *dual* when referring to two items.) Case refers to the grammatical role the noun plays in the sentence with regard to the verb or other nouns. In English we typically distinguish between the *subject* case and the *object* case. For example,

I see the boy/him. (*The boy* is the object of the verb.)
The boy/he sees me. (*The boy* is the subject of the verb.)

The noun phrase "the boy" doesn't change its form depending on its grammatical role, but the pronouns I/me and he/him change their shape depending on their role. Latin distinguishes six cases and signals a change in role by a change in ending:

nominative	puella	equus	mīles
genitive	puellae	equī	mīlitis
dative	puellae	equō	mīlitī
accusative	puellam	equum	mīlitem
ablative	puellā	equō	mīlite
vocative	puella	eque	mīles

In languages where the shapes of pronouns, determiners, and adjectives change according to the nouns they modify or replace, the pronoun, determiner, or adjective can also be described as to gender, number, and case. (In English, for example, *this* is singular; *these* is plural. *He* is nominative singular, masculine; *her* is accusative singular feminine.)

Verbs can be described in terms of *person, number, tense,* and *voice.*

Person refers to the subject—the first person is the narrator (*I/we*); the second person is the person spoken to (*you,* singular or plural); the third person is the person or thing spoken about (*he/she/it/they*). Number refers to whether the subject is singular or plural. In English the shape of the verb changes only when the subject is third-person singular (*I work, he/she/it works*), but note the differences in other languages:

	French	*German*	*Latin*	*English*
(1st/sing.)	je travaille	ich arbeite	labōrō	(I work)
(2nd/sing.)	tu travailles	du arbeitst	labōrās	(you work)
(3rd/sing.)	il travaille	er arbeite	labōrat	(he works)

Tense refers to where the action is situated in relation to now. In English we distinguish present, past, and future tenses, which can be simple, compound, or progressive. Note that the French form **je parle** or the German **ich spreche** represents three possible translations in English: "I speak, I do speak, I am speaking."

Voice refers to whether the action of the verb is

performed by the subject or whether it is performed on the subject. For example, in the sentences:

The hunter shot the bear.
The bear was shot by the hunter.

While both sentences mean the same, in the first sentence the verb is *active* because the subject performs the action, while in the second sentence the verb is *passive* because the action of shooting is performed on the subject.

In addition verbs can be classified as *transitive* (i.e., capable of taking an object) or *intransitive* (i.e., not taking an object.) Examples of transitive verbs in English are: to eat, to hit, to find. Examples of intransitive verbs are: to arrive, to sleep, to fall.

SAMPLE GRAMMAR EXERCISES

Knowledge of grammar entails the ability to understand and use the linguistic markers that signal tense, voice, and person in verbs and gender and number in nouns and pronouns.

Your knowledge of the grammar of the target language will be tested in the classroom, on homework, and on tests (teacher-made and standardized) by various types of exercises. With any type of exercise (as you are taught in preparing for the SATs) the key to success is understanding what is being tested by the exercise. Thus, with grammar exercises, you need to know what aspect of grammar is being tested and how you are expected to show an understanding of the grammar construction. Different types of exercises will be used, some more appropriate to a particular structure than others.

What follows is a sample of types of exercises you may encounter and some hints as to how to understand what is being tested and how to do them successfully. (For these examples of grammar exercises, the directions will be in English. However, many textbooks and workbooks use the target language for directions as early as possible.)

1. Rewrite the noun phrase by adding the adjectives in parentheses:

[French]	(petit, français)	la voiture
[Spanish]	(facil, español)	cinco libros
[Italian]	(grande, italiano)	i ragazzi
[German]	(schwarz, gross)	eine Katze

For languages such as French, Spanish, or Italian, in which the form of the adjective varies according to the noun it modifies, you will have to analyze the gender (masculine or feminine) and number (singular or plural) of the noun in order to determine the form of the adjective. Then you must determine *where* the adjective occurs in relation to the noun. In French, Spanish, and Italian most adjectives occur after the noun but some occur before the noun. In German, all the adjectives occur before the noun. For example, in the Italian example, **ragazzi** is masculine plural, and **grande** becomes **grandi; italiano** becomes **italiani. Grandi** goes *before* the noun; **italiani,** *after* the noun. So the answer is

i grandi ragazzi italiani.

2. Fill in the blanks using the correct form of the possessive that agrees with the subject:

[French]	Nous cherchons_____livres.
[German]	Wollen Sie nicht mit_____Eltern sprechen?
[Italian]	La ragazza cerca_____fratello.
[Spanish]	Los chicos no tienen_____libros.

For this exercise you must not only make sure that you choose the possessive that corresponds with the subject, but you must make sure that the possessive agrees in gender and number with the noun it modifies. Thus, in the Italian example, it is the subject **La ragazza** that determines that the possessive must be the third-person singular (that is, one of **suo/sua/sui/sue**) and the modified **fratello**, which requires the masculine singular form **suo**.

3. Scrambled Sentences. Unscramble the following words and put them into the correct order to form a complete sentence:

[German] heute / möchte / machen / mein / ich / Arbeit
[Italian] domani / andare / non / cinema / possiamo / al
[Spanish] estudiantes / inglés / profesor / con / el / los / habla
[French] avons / hier / nous / le / soir / pas / film / vu / n'

You'll need to attack this exercise in two steps. First, identify which words go together. For example, in the German sentence the masculine singular possessive **mein** goes with the masculine singular noun **Arbeit**. Secondly, you should identify the verb and decide by its ending what the subject must be. In the German sentence **möchte** is the first-person singular form of the verb, so the only subject could be **ich.** Furthermore, does this verb take a direct object, indirect object, both, or neither; can it introduce another verb or clause? Thirdly, you must know the correct order in which the subject, verb, direct object, indirect object, prepositional phrases, and secondary verbs occur in the target language. For example, in French, Spanish, and Italian, direct-object noun phrases occur after the verb, but the pronouns that replace them go before the verb. In the German example, the secondary verb, **machen**, would come last:

Ich **möchte** mein Arbeit heute machen.

4. In the blank space write the correct form of the present tense of the verb in parentheses:

[Italian] Le ragazze (parlare)_____al professore.
[German] Wohin (gehen)_____das Mädchen?
[French] Pourquoi (regarder)_____-tu ce film?
[Spanish] Yo no (tener)_____el dinero conmigo.

You will need to determine the person and number of the subject of the sentence in order to decide which ending of the verb to choose so that the subject and verb agree. For example, in the German example the subject, **das Mäd-chen**, is third-person singular, so the verb ending must be **-t**. So the correct answer is

Wohin geht das Mädchen?

5. The following words are in the correct order. Expand them into a complete sentence, adding the definite article to each noun and putting the verb in the present tense:

[German]	**wann / können / du / zu / Kino / morgen / kommen**
[French]	**mère / montrer / photos / à / petit / garçon**
[Italian]	**sua / amica / cantare / con / gruppo / famoso**
[Spanish]	**estudiantes / querer / aprender / palabras**

You need to determine the gender and number of each noun in order to use the correct form of the definite article, and the person and number of the subject of the sentence in order to make sure that the verb's ending agrees. The answer to the Spanish example would be

Los estudiantes quieren aprender las palabras.

6. Rewrite the following sentences, replacing the underlined noun phrase with the appropriate pronoun:

[French] Mon frère ne va pas voir les films.
[Spanish] La cliente compra pantalones.
[German] Die Jungen sehen den Zug nicht.

You will need to determine the role: subject/direct object/ indirect object; the gender: masculine or feminine; and the number: singular or plural of the noun phrase to be replaced in order to choose the correct pronouns. For example, with the French sentence, **Mon frère** is a masculine singular subject and is replaced by **il**; **les films** is a masculine plural direct object and is replaced by **les**. You also need to determine where the pronouns go in relation to the verb. So the correct answer is

il ne va pas les voir.

7. The following statements are answers to questions. Change them into questions by replacing the underlined phrases into interrogative words.

[German] Elke geht nach Hause.
[Italian] I nostri amici arrivano domani mattina.
[French] Nous avons acheté nos vélos à Paris.
[Spanish] Los chicos llegan domingo.

For this type of exercise you need to analyze the meaning and the grammatical role of the underlined phrase in order to determine which of the interrogative words (i.e., the target language equivalents of who(m)/ what/when/where/why/ how) is appropriate. Secondly, the word order for a statement must be changed to the word order for a question. Thus, for the German example, the phrase **nach Hause** ("(to) home") would answer the question word **Wohin** ("(to) where"); for the question form the verb and subject are *inverted*. So, the correct answer is

Wohin geht Elke?

8. Fill in the blanks in the following sentences, using the correct form of the verb:

[Italian] Quando avró abbastanza denaro, (andare) _____nel Ticino.

[French] Si j'avais assez d'argent, j' (aller)_____en France.

[German] Als wir das Kino verliessen, (regnen)_____es.

[Latin] Rogabant ubi dux (esse)_____

For this type of exercise you must identify the clue words that signal a particular rule. For example, in the Italian sentence the conjunction **Quando** followed by the future tense of the verb, **avró**, requires that the future form of the verb, **andró**, be used in the main clause.)

9. Combine each of the following pairs of simple sentences to form compound sentences by using the appropriate relative pronoun:

[French] Voici enfin mes gants. Je les cherche depuis trois jours.

[German] Wo ist mein Buch? Ich muss es lesen.

[Italian] Dove sono i miei libri? Li ho lasciati nella biblioteca.

For this type of exercise you need to identify what the two sentences have in common, decide which noun phrase or pronoun you're going to replace with a relative pronoun, and determine its role in order to decide which relative pronoun to use. For example, in the French example, **les** in the second sentence refers to **mes gants**; as the direct object, **les** would be replaced by **que** to yield:

Voici enfin mes gants que je cherche depuis trois jours.

10. Change the following sentences containing direct quotes into indirect speech:

[French] Ma sœur m'a dit: "Je n'ai plus faim."
[German] Mein Freund hat mir gesagt: "Ich will den Film sehen."
[Italian] Luigi mi ha detto: "Mia sorella deve andare alla farmacia."

With this type of exercise you must analyze the relation of the subject in the quote to the main part of the sentence, and of the tense of the verb in the quote to the main verb. In the Italian sentence **Mia sorella** refers to Luigi's sister, so **Mia** becomes **sua;** the verb **deve** is in the present tense in the quotation but must change to a past tense to become synchronous with the main verb, **ha detto,** so it becomes **doveva;** and the conjunction **che** is used to introduce the secondary clause:

Luigi mi ha detto che sua sorella doveva andare alla farmacia.

HINTS AND SUGGESTIONS

Following are a few hints to keep in mind as you study the particular features of the grammar of another language.

Don't be afraid to make mistakes. Your English teacher will probably tell you that you make a few mistakes in English. That doesn't stop you from speaking and writing English. Believe it or not, speakers of the language you are learning also make grammatical mistakes, but keep right on using the language. Develop an attitude that you are going to make yourself understood, somehow, in spite of a lack of vocabulary or grammatical mistakes. This doesn't mean that you should ignore grammar rules or use nonsense vocabulary, but not using a language until you're absolutely sure you can use it perfectly will only mean that you'll never get started. And in this area, success breeds success. That is, being able to make yourself understood will encourage you to use the language more.

The grammar of the language you are studying is logical for that language from that language's point of view. It may not appear to follow the logic of English, so you should not try to compare structures of operations of a foreign language with those of English. Instead of asking "Why do they do it this way in German, French, Russian, etc.?" (to which your teacher may respond "Because. . . ."), try to understand the rationale behind the grammatical rule or structure.

Transfer concepts you have already learned in English; nouns, verbs, adjectives, adverbs, prepositions, conjunctions often function like similar parts of speech from one language to the next.

Use formulas and charts to help you solve the mystery of grammatical structures: For example, a noun phrase (NP) in French could be analyzed according to the following formula:

NP ⇒ Det + (Aj) + N + (Aj)
      ↓   ↓   ↓   ↓
      Le   petit garçon français

which is a lot easier to understand than "a noun phrase is made up of a determiner followed by an optional adjective of the type that precedes the noun, followed by a noun, followed by an optional adjective of the type that follows the noun."

Before you are able to reel off a French sentence containing a negative and a couple of object pronouns, it might help if you could visualize the order with a formula like the following:

SENT ⇒ Subj + (ne) + ObjPn + Verb + (pas) + NP
      ↓   ↓   ↓   ↓   ↓   ↓
    Je   ne   lui   prêterai pas   mon vélo.

A particular problem in learning a foreign language often has to do with which verb tense to use. It may be helpful to use a "time chart," which enables you to visualize which tense is appropriate:

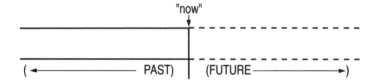

Use analysis and analogy: for example, if the stem of the French verb, **parler** is **parl-**, and the stem of the verb **donner** is **donn-**, and the stem of **écouter** is **écout-**, then you can probably figure out that the stem of **regarder** is **regard-**. If you know for example that in German the past participle of the verb typically occurs last in the sentence and ends in **-en**, you can probably construct a new sentence based on a pattern you have already learned. Indeed, pattern practice is a teaching/learning strategy that can be employed to reinforce the grammatical patterns you are learning. (When you start figuring out these operations by yourself, the foreign language will suddenly seem a lot less foreign.)

FOUR

LEARNING TO LISTEN AND COMPREHEND IN A FOREIGN LANGUAGE

The first linguistic skill necessary for fluency in another language is the passive aural skill of **listening comprehension**, which involves the decoding of the stream of foreign sounds you hear, being able to distinguish between them and group them into meaningful, understandable units. Right now you are probably asking yourself the big question: "How am I ever going to be able to understand what someone is saying in Spanish/French/German/Italian/Russian/Chinese/Japanese/Arabic . . . especially when it sounds as if they're speaking at a million miles an hour?"

The answer to that question is that listening comprehension is a gradual process, sometimes a bit slow, but one that is marked by sudden, large leaps in your ability to understand. People who learn other languages often speak of moving from lower to higher "plateaus" in their ability to understand a foreign language. Trust me, it will happen.

You need to realize and appreciate that each language has its own stock of sounds and also has specific ways in which these sounds may combine. Remember that all languages do not use the same sounds or allow sounds to occur in the same combinations. Listening comprehension means being able to decipher (that is, tune your ear to decipher) the sounds, combinations of sounds, intonation, and stress patterns of the language you are learning.

Your first step in understanding the target language involves training your ear to distinguish the specific phonemes (i.e., the meaningful units of sound) of that language. With regard to the sounds that occur in a foreign language compared to those that occur in English, we can distinguish three general categories:

1. sounds that are the same in both the foreign language and English;
2. sounds that occur in English, but do not occur in the foreign language;
3. sounds that occur in the foreign language but do not occur in English.

The second category of sounds will present no problem for you. (For example, the sounds represented by the letters **th** in **then** or **with** are two sounds that do not occur in French. However, for this same reason, they present special problems for the speaker of French who is learning English.)

With the first category of sounds (namely, those occurring in both English and in the language you are studying) you must also realize that similar sounds may have a different *distribution* in a different language. Distribution refers to where a particular sound or group of sounds occur in the syllable—i.e., at the beginning, in the middle, or at the end of the syllable. For example, the sound represented by **ng** never occurs in initial syllable position in English; it occurs in final or medial position: as in **song, bring, anger, singing**. However, in Vietnamese it also occurs in syllable initial position, as in **Nguyen**, and this position will cause a problem for the speaker of English. The sound represented by **ge** in

gara*ge,* lie*ge*—both words of French origin—occurs only in final position in English, but it also occurs in initial position, as in **géographie, *j*ambon**, in French; again, this position may cause difficulty for the English speaker.

The third category of sounds, i.e., those that do not occur in English but do occur in the foreign language, require that special attention be paid to the individual sound and how it differs from English sounds that may at first seem "similar" to you. For example, the nasal vowels of French do not occur in English. They present particular problems for the English speaker to hear, distinguish, and reproduce them. However similar they may seem to the ears of the English speaker they are different phonemes and cannot be confused.

> **DANS** /dã/ means "in"
> **D'UN** /dœ̃/ means "of a"
> **DONT** /dõ/ means "whose"

The greatest "danger" comes from sounds that are similar to those of English, but are not the same. If you cannot train your ear to distinguish the differences between sounds or, worse, if you try to "translate" them into a similar sound in English, you run the risk of never being able to make meaningful distinctions. (Beware of phrase books that offer "English equivalent" pronunciations for sounds that don't occur in English.)

You're right, of course, to feel that listening comprehension is a difficult skill to master, that it will take a long time for you to understand everything that a native speaker of a language says. The difficulty lies in the fact that you cannot control the speed or the manner of the native speaker. However, you need to realize that languages are *redundant*; that they give more clues than are absolutely necessary for the speaker to transmit, or the listener to decode, ideas. For example, let's say you get a phone call from a friend and because of the music from your stereo you only catch this much of what she says:

"What'd_____get_____th's test?"

You may still be able to respond because you've picked up enough signals from the vocabulary, morphology, intonation, spacing, and context (i.e., who's calling when and why) to figure out that your friend asked:

"What'd you get on Mr. Smith's test?"

(Linguists tell us that we can decode messages in our own language while receiving only half of the total message.) However, there is a real difference in the degree of redundancy for us between English and an unfamiliar language. So, we must really pay attention to the speaker and look for clues, visual or contextual.

Just as in decoding your friend's garbled message you focused on the ideas being transmitted, so it is important to understand that being able to comprehend what is being said is essentially *understanding the ideas.*

You will not learn to comprehend another language by trying to isolate and translate every single word you hear. You will never be able to keep up if you try this, and will only experience frustration. You will be able to comprehend when you learn to *listen for ideas,* meaningful units composed of groups of words that may also be separated by pauses, especially when the speaker is trying to help you understand. The person with whom you're speaking may even try to reinforce ideas with hand gestures.

Your ability to understand the spoken target language will come in stages. At first everything will seem to be run together; then you will be able to hear distinct words; next, you will be able to separate ideas made up of groups of words, understanding most of what is said; finally, you will be able to understand everything that is said without having to strain to hear it.

Being able to comprehend what you hear in a conversation with another person or in a small group requires *active listening.* This means that you must pay close attention to what the speaker is saying. (The less fluent you are in the target language, the more attention you need to pay.) Listen for key words that signal the general topic of the conversation and look for visual clues in the gestures of the speaker(s).

Active listening also means giving feedback to your interlocutor (the person with whom you are having a conversation). You should nod to show that you understand or interject a phrase such as "I see," "You're right," "Yes, that's true." Conversely, if you don't understand, let the speaker know by furrowing your brow or saying "How's that?"

OTHER OPPORTUNITIES FOR LISTENING

Modern technology provides additional opportunities for the student to hear the target language used by native speakers. Most of the larger cities in the United States have radio stations that broadcast in Spanish. Other cities have occasional programs in different languages that serve the various resident ethnic communities. A shortwave radio is your passport to dozens of languages and countries around the world. Tune in to a program broadcast in the language you are studying and let it play music, news, chatter, whatever, while you are doing other things.

Let your ear and mind get used to the sound of the language. It's not necessary for you to understand everything you hear. Just relax and get the feel for the language sounds. You can do the same with language cassettes available through the mail or in bookstores. Then there is cable television, which typically offers a channel in Spanish (or in French if you are close enough to Quebec). Or the next time you go to your local video store, look for the foreign-language films instead of checking out another Teenage Mutant Ninja Turtles. Avoid dubbed films and pick those with the original sound tracks or with subtitles. It's all right to look at the subtitles while watching the movie; just make sure that you are listening closely to the dialogue. Use the context of the film, the visual clues, to help you understand what is happening.

LISTENING COMPREHENSION EXERCISES
1. Listen to the following sentences and indicate whether the sentence is about Michel, a boy, by writing G (for *garçon*) or about Michelle, a girl, by writing JF (for *jeune fille*):

Michel est petit.
Michelle est curieuse.

With this type of exercise you will need to be able to hear the distinction between the masculine form and the feminine form of the adjective that is the only aural clue for differentiating between Michel and Michelle, since they are pronounced the same.

2. Listen to the following sentences and indicate whether the subject **Sie** is singular (i.e., "she") or plural (i.e., "they"):

Sie ist sehr schön.
Sind sie pünktlich?
Sie hat kein Geld.
Haben sie mein Buch?

With this type of exercise you must be able to hear the difference between the singular form and the plural form of the verb, signaled by a difference in the verb's ending because **sie** can mean either "she" or "they."

3. Listen first to the following dialogue and then decide whether the statements that follow it are true or false:

> **[Maria:] Ciao, Luigi. Come vai?**
> **[Luigi:] Abbastanza bene, ma sono stanco.**
> **[Maria:] Stanco, ma perché?**
> **[Luigi:] Perché ho molto da fare per la scuola.**
> **[Maria:] Vuoi andare al cinema con Paola e me?**
> **[Luigi:] Scusi, ma non posso. Devo finire il mio lavoro stasera.**

As you become increasingly more fluent in the target language, you will listen to longer passages and will then be expected to respond to questions (written or oral) about the information contained in the passage.

Dictations are also a favorite method for testing listening comprehension (and writing ability). You will have to be able to decode the spoken passage, separating the various ideas into the words that constitute them, and spell them correctly.

HINTS AND SUGGESTIONS

When you are listening in order to practice pronunciation, *listen carefully to the individual sound while looking at your teacher's face.* Note how his/her mouth is shaped and *listen to the description of how this "foreign" sound is produced.* (Where is the tongue placed? Are the lips rounded? Are the lips touching? How is the air flow interrupted?) Often charts showing the shape of the mouth, and position of tongue and lips are available to help you practice how a sound is produced.

You need to recognize that the sounds of the language you are studying must be pronounced correctly. Coming "close" (unlike in horseshoes) does not count and can lead to confusion. (I am sure that you know of examples in English where the change of one sound in a word or phrase leads to confusion and embarrassment. Lots of jokes are based on the confusion of "close" sounds.) A very important word of advice is to avoid the temptation to say to yourself, "It sort of sounds like_____in English." Doing so will only cause confusion and you will end up pronouncing the foreign sound incorrectly.

Back in chapter 1 we saw the example of how you could spell *fish* GHOTI if you pronounced those letters a certain way. Well, this is just another way of warning you: *Do not confuse sounds with letters.* A particular *written* letter does not always represent the same sound. (In English, and some other languages, there is not always a close correspondence between sounds and their written symbols, letters.) In English the letters *ough* are pronounced six different ways in the following words: *bough, rough, cough, ought, though, through.* In Spanish the *d* of **dos** sounds like the *d* of English *day* while the *d* of **lado** (which occurs between two vowels) sounds like the *th* of English *they.* The *th* sound of either *with* or *thin* does not even occur in Spanish or Italian; in French the letter combination *th* occurs in such words as **thé** or **cathédrale** but it is pronounced like the *t* of *tea.*

Keep a list of words that contain a particular sound you are trying to master. That way you can practice pronunciation as you commit the words to memory. It would be to your advantage to take the time to learn the phonemic symbols for the sounds of the language you are studying. The advantage of this tactic is that you can group together a number of words as containing a particular sound you have trouble recognizing or reproducing. For example, the French words **dans, en, remplir, sang** all contain the nasal vowel /ã/, which doesn't occur in English. Group together words that contain a "difficult" sound and practice listening for and reproducing this sound.

When listening to and following a written passage that is being read aloud, *try to generalize about the pronunciation of a sound*; if the letter *e* topped by a circumflex accent (ˆ) is pronounced a certain way the first three times you hear it, then **ê** will probably be pronounced the same way the fourth time. You will note that German **ü** is pronounced differently from **u**. You might even make a list of words that contain one of the sounds and practice first one list, then the other, then go back and forth between the two lists.

Listen for differences in intonation that can carry a difference in meaning. For example, the difference in French between the question **Tu parles français?** and the statement **Tu parles français** will be signaled in speech by a rise in intonation at the end of the sentence to signal the question and a falling off of intonation to signal the statement.

In listening for comprehension, *look for clues in the context*. Much of speech is inspired by something visual. Many teachers of language use an **audio-visual** (that is, sound-sight) approach to language teaching. If you keep your eyes and ears open and remain attentive, what you hear may make sense with what you see. (This oftens happens when you are watching a movie and don't catch what one of the actors said, but you can figure it out from what is happening.) Speech is often closely tied to the context because the context may be the inspiration for the speech.

Listen for words and phrases you have heard be-

fore. Teachers build new ideas on top of what you have already learned. For example, there are generally two types of questions: yes/no questions and specific word (who/what/when/where/why) questions. The yes/no questions your teacher poses will probably involve vocabulary and ideas you've been reading about or discussing. A yes/no question (signaled by rising intonation) asks you to assess whether the information in the question is true or not. Thus, to respond to such a question you need only to repeat the essential information, preceding it with the word for yes or no, and making the verb negative if you've answered no.

It is very important to *relax.* Don't try to figure out every single sound that you hear. If one slips by, you'll get it next time. Don't worry if you miss a word or two. Sometimes, the context will help you decipher their meaning.

One day you will find that you have passed to an even higher level where groups of sounds, in longer and longer stretches, make lights go off in your head. Congratulations, you are at the level of understanding ideas and groups of ideas. Press on. This is what you have been working for.

FIVE

LEARNING TO SPEAK A FOREIGN LANGUAGE

The linguistic skill of speaking a foreign language is closely related to that of listening comprehension, and as with listening comprehension, you develop this skill in stages, moving from the production of individual sounds and sound clusters to words and finally phrases. Speaking a foreign language is certainly more than simply parroting what you hear. It is an active skill and involves producing your own ideas freely in speech, reacting to various stimuli in what you hear, see, or read.

By now, you must be asking yourself the big question: "How am I ever going to be able to make myself understood in Chinese/Arabic/French/German/Spanish/Japanese/Italian . . . by someone who has been speaking it his entire life?" Well, don't worry, you will get there with a bit of patience and persistence. It is also important to realize that you won't have to learn to speak French or German well enough to discuss world politics with a busy waiter in a Berlin café full of demanding customers. At least, not yet. You will be learning to speak in a classroom filled with other anxious students like yourself, working with a teacher who is eager that you make progress and feel a sense of accomplishment. You will also be pleasantly surprised by the warm, helpful attitude of native speakers of the language you are studying when you first use your new language with them. Just watch the smiles light up! (In his book, *Stealing from a Deep Place,* author Brian Hill recounts the first time he used the only three words he knew in Bulgarian, **"Ne studeno; dobur."** [No cold; good."] to explain how by cycling he was managing to stay warm in the cold weather. But he managed to make himself understood to his interlocutors and came away from this experience with a sense of accomplishment.)

The ideal way of learning to speak a foreign language involves total immersion, being in a situation where one is forced to use the target language because the target language is the only means of communication. At the boarding school in Switzerland where the author was headmaster, students for whom English was a second (or third or fourth) language had to use English in the classroom and in the dormitories to communicate. Off campus, however, Italian was the *lingua franca* for all students who needed it to communicate with shopkeepers, bus drivers, and neighbors.

Within the structured learning environment of a foreign language class you will be led from listening to your teacher and repeating what your teacher says, to using phrases in appropriate situations, to answering questions, to longer forms of less guided speech. Your ultimate goal of speaking freely in the foreign language will be attained after much trial and error, at the end of many intermediary steps.

To return to the analogy of learning to ride a bike, or playing tennis, or making shots in basketball, we realize that feeling comfortable on a ten-speeder, or at hitting a backhand, or making a reverse lay-up comes as the result of hours of practice. Speaking a foreign language is also a *skill* that must be practiced over and over until it becomes second nature to you. You learn to speak another language by speaking it whenever you can, by finding occasions to use it.

One of the biggest roadblocks to overcome will be your own inhibitions. Don't be afraid to use gestures to try to communicate your ideas. In order to pronounce a language correctly you may have to produce "strange" sounds that don't occur in English. Your teacher will tell you how to pronounce those sounds (for example, the vowel sound represented by **u** of French **lu, tu, du** is pronounced by putting the tip of the tongue behind the teeth and rounding the lips), but if you don't follow the directions (in this case because you don't want to "pucker up") you'll never pronounce the sound correctly.

So, how about carrying on a "conversation" with yourself in the shower, without the fear of being corrected, just to get used to the "feel" of trying the language. Practice pronunciation or reading a passage with a friend, just so you can have an audience, a friendly listener. Yes, you may make mistakes, which your teacher will catch and correct, but you will also be one step closer to feeling more comfortable with using the language.

TYPES OF SPEAKING EXERCISES

1. The first type of exercise you are likely to encounter will be pronunciation exercises, usually focusing on the production of a particular sound that may or may not be contained in spoken English. Typically, you will repeat after the teacher a series of words (written in your text) that contain the sound. For example:

[German] do<u>ch</u>, Bu<u>ch</u>, ma<u>ch</u>en, brau<u>ch</u>e
[French] v<u>u</u>, s<u>u</u>perbe, r<u>u</u>e, l<u>u</u>nette

[Italian] c̲erco, c̲i, c̲ento, c̲erto
[Spanish] piña̲, cañ̲on, niñ̲o

You will need to pay particular attention to the teacher's directions for producing the sound and listen and watch closely as your teacher produces it. Also, you should note if this sound is signaled by a particular letter or group of letters or by a diacritical mark.

2. A second type of exercise involves pronouncing contrasting *minimal pairs* that is, words that differ by a single sound (that makes for the difference in meaning). For example:

[Italian] passo/pazzo; tassa/tazza
[Spanish] buro/burro; pero/perro
[French] corps/cœur; sort/sœur; lors/leur

You must learn to hear and focus on producing the exact sound because what is, to you, a slight difference in sound may completely change the meaning.

3. *Pattern practice* involves beginning with a particular grammatical construction or pattern and then making substitutions in order to produce new sentences. For example:

[German]	Der Zug kommt bald.	nicht
	Der Zug kommt nicht.	Die Strassenbahn
	Die Strassenbahn kommt nicht.	jetzt
	Die Strassenbahn kommt jetzt.	geht
	Die Strassenbahn geht jetzt.	
[French]	Nous allons au cinéma ce soir.	demain
	Nous allons au cinéma demain.	au zoo
	Nous allons au zoo demain.	à la boulangerie
	Nous allons à la boulangerie demain.	Ma mère
	Ma mère va à la boulangerie demain.	
[Italian]	Mia madre parla italiano.	inglese
	Mia madre parla inglese.	Mia sorella

Mia sorella parla inglese.	tedesco
Mia sorella parla tedesco.	I miei amici
I miei amici parlano tedesco.	

You need to understand the role of the item you are replacing in relation to the other parts of the sentence. Thus, in the Italian example, **i miei amici** is the new subject, replacing **Mia sorella**, and requires a verb that is third-person plural; in this case, **parla** must become **parlano**.

4. Sometimes you will practice repeating long utterances by first breaking them down into shorter meaningful units, separated by pauses, then "rebuilding" the sentences. For example:

[German] Zuerst / muss ich / das Buch lesen // dann kanne ich / zu die Eisdiele mitkommen.

[French] Ma petite sœur / est allée / à la boulangerie // òu elle a acheté / du pain.

[Italian] Non posso andare / al cinema con te // perché ho troppo da fare / per la scuola domani.

[Spanish] Mis amigos / van al cine // porque hay / una buena película.

The important point here is to keep meaningful units intact in order not to fracture the string of ideas. As confidence builds you will be able to string shorter phrases together into longer ones. However, you must think in terms of ideas, not words.

A lot of speech is **reactive.** This means that you are required to *respond* to something you see, hear, or read. Quite often, you are asked to respond to questions your teacher asks you in class. Let me give you a few hints to help you overcome your natural fear of saying the wrong thing or not knowing how to get started.

Basically, there are just two types of questions: yes/

no questions and specific interrogative-word questions. Here are yes/no questions:

TEACHER: **Hans sprecht Deutsch?**
¿Juan habla español?
Jean parle français?
Giovanni parla italiano?

For this type of question the basic response your teacher is looking for is yes/no, **ja/nein, si/no, oui/non.** So listen closely to the question and *attack it in two stages.* First decide if the content of the question is true or false (i.e., does Jean speak the language, or not) and answer the equivalent of "yes" or "no." Then repeat the core of the question. For example,

TEACHER: **¿Juan habla español?**
YOU: (1) **Si.**
          (2) **Si, Juan habla español.**

The second type of question is a specific interrogative word (who/what/when/where/why/how?) question. For example, you hear

TEACHER: <u>Where</u> is Marie going?
<u>Où</u> va Marie?
<u>Wohin</u> geht Maria?
<u>Dove</u> va Maria?

To produce an answer to this type of question, you also want to attack it in two stages. First listen to the entire question and figure out the answer to the specific interrogative word (i.e., "Where . . . ?"—". . . to the cathedral."). So give the answer to the specific interrogative word, then repeat the core of the question, adding your specific answer to it. For example,

TEACHER: **Dove va Maria?**
YOU: (1) **Al duomo.**
            (2) **Maria va al duomo.**

HINTS AND SUGGESTIONS

When you are practicing pronunciation, whether of in-dividual sounds, or of longer words and phrases, it is most important that you *do not try to make the foreign language sound into the nearest sound in English.* Each language has its own group of sounds, intona-tion, and stress patterns, which may be very different from those of English. If you try to make everything "comfortable" for yourself, you will only wind up sound-ing like an American trying to speak another language.

Beware of cognates that differ not only in terms of the pronunciation of individual sounds but also in terms of stress. For example, the Spanish word **posibilidad** is stressed on the last syllable, unlike English *possibility.* Unlike its English cognate *geography*, which receives primary stress on the second syllable, French **géo-graphie** has the same amount of stress on each sylla-ble (although the last syllable is slightly longer).

Don't let the lack of a specific vocabulary item keep you from trying to make yourself understood. Occa-sionally, you can start the sentence and let your listener finish it for you, perhaps even aiding him/her along with a hand gesture. For example, let's say that you don't know the German word for "stamp." You show your paper and envelope to the other person and point to the spot where the stamp would go as you say:

Ich habe Papier und einen Umschlag. Ich brauche ein . . .

Body language and gestures can play a very important role in conveying a message to your listener. Take every opportunity, particularly when you are first trying to express yourself in the foreign language, to use your hands to point, to make shapes, and to generally "describe" what you are conveying orally.

Learn a few stock phrases in the foreign language that will enable you to proceed with what you already know or to get out of a "tight spot." Such phrases should include the foreign language equivalent for:

How do you say_____?
What does_____mean?
Please repeat.
Slowly, please.
I don't understand.
Do you mean_____?

It is important to realize that while the stream of speech can be broken down into individual sounds, language is essentially the transmission of ideas. When you speak, in English or your adopted language, you are trying to communicate one or more ideas that you have in your mind to a listener. So here are a few hints about speaking freely.

When speaking to be understood, relax and go slowly. *Try to group your words into* **idea units** *and pause after each one of these units.* It is not necessary to speak at a hundred miles an hour to make yourself understood or even to be considered fluent. Fluency has more to do with being understood than speed. For example, the following sentence in English is made up of four ideas that can be separated from one another by slight pauses without affecting either the speaker's fluency or the listener's ability to understand:

The little boy / can't find / the French book / that you were reading.

Now, let's say that you are trying to articulate the same sentence in French. If, instead of stumbling along word by word or trying to blurt out the whole sentence and winding up leaving out a couple of words, you were to attack it **idea by idea**, pausing after each idea:

Le petit garçon / ne peut pas trouver / le livre français / que tu lisais,

you will not only be easily understood but you will have the confident sense of being able to communicate your ideas.

Of course, the idea may come to you first in English. A certain amount of translation takes place even with advanced speakers of a language other than their own. Perhaps you hear the question in German but you unwittingly translate it into English, then find yourself arriving at the answer in English and trying to frame your response in German. Don't worry, there will come a day when the answer will come to you almost automatically in German, and then think how much mental energy you will be saving.

It is nearly impossible to attain any degree of fluency in another language if your use of language is limited to less than an hour a day in the classroom. So, you need to take every opportunity you can to use the language both in the classroom and outside. Some suggestions:

Join the French/Spanish/German/Latin club at school. This will give you the opportunity to use the language in a less stressful situation than the classroom, where you are working for a grade. You'll get the opportunity to explore the language in a different situation than through a textbook, with magazines, music, and movies.

Set up a French/Spanish/German/Latin table at

lunch so you can use the language in an everyday situation.

Become a host for an exchange student. This will give you the opportunity to use the language intensively in everyday situations. All right, maybe your exchange student will want to use only English, but you can work out a compromise: one day only English, the next day only the other language. Or perhaps you use only the other language and your exchange student uses only English; and you can correct one another's usage.

Listen to and sing along with cassettes in the language you are studying. This helps to build vocabulary and will help with your pronunciation. It will also put you more at ease with the language.

After you've practiced those new sentences in your morning shower "conversation," try them out on your teacher in class later in the day.

In summary, try using the phrases and vocabulary you have been learning in class in any suitable situation. For example, a simple **"Das Brot, bitte"** at the lunch table can be a pleasant alternative to saying "Pass me the bread, please" for the millionth time. Take every opportunity to "try the language on" in order to become comfortable with how the language sounds coming off your tongue.

Then comes that magic day when you know that you are on the edge of fluency, when you wake up and realize that you have been dreaming in the foreign language. Maybe it was just a dream of your teacher asking you a question in the language, but this time you understood perfectly and had no trouble coming up with an answer, and it seemed so natural to do so! Congratulations.

VOCABULARY BUILDING

Semantics is another of the subsystems of language. Semantics deals with the relationship between words and the items or ideas to which they refer. In this chapter we will discuss the acquisition of vocabulary in a foreign language and how we expand our bank of vocabulary items.

Language is symbolic. This means that **/teybəl/**in English, **/tablə/** in French, **/tavolə/** in Italian or whatever group of sounds another language uses to represent

is not the thing or idea itself, but only stands for the thing.

Taking a scenario from our earlier tale of prehistoric man, we can imagine one day when our hero Oog caught his first glance of a new animal and excitedly tapped his hunting partner Zoog on the shoulder. "Hey, Zoog, what's that over there? Never saw one of them before." And Zoog, the smarter of the two, replied, "Don't know. Guess we'll have to name it. Let's call it a 'quiboxer.' " A different hunting group hundreds or thousands of miles away may have named the new creature a "ztarpo."

CULTURAL DIFFERENCES

Greek philosophers debated the relationship between an object in nature (**physos**) and the word used to refer to it (**nomos**). While some felt that the relationship between the vocabulary item and the thing was fixed and necessary, others felt that the relationship is arbitrary. (Which point of view do you think is correct?)

When speakers of English see a they use the word *dog*; French speakers say **chien**, Italian speakers say **cane**, and speakers of German use the word **Hund**.

So, who is correct? Which is the correct word for this object? The answer is that all are correct in their own language because the relationship between the vocabulary item and the thing that it represents is *arbitrary*, that is, there is no necessity that the thing be called a certain way, named with only one word. Whatever the speakers decide to use in order to name an item is up to them. By their agreement, the relationship between the vocabulary item and the thing is *conventional.*

Some languages make distinctions that are not culturally significant in other languages. For example, speakers of Latin made the distinction between **avunculus** ("uncle who is the mother's brother") and **patruus** ("uncle who is the father's brother"), while languages derived from Latin do not make this distinction. That is, there is only one word for "uncle" in Italian (**zio**), French (**oncle**), and Spanish (**tio**).

We may make a mistaken assumption that there is a single precise word in a foreign language for each word in English and, conversely, each word we learn in the foreign language can be translated by a single word in English. This is not so. Perhaps this is easier to understand if we realize that many words in English have a number of different meanings. For example, the word *run* can be a verb meaning: (1) to run in a race or (2) to run a business or a meeting; or it can be a noun, (3) what you score in a baseball game. *Walk* can be a verb that is either intransitive ("I walk to school every day.") or transitive ("I walk my dog each day.") or a noun ("Let's take a walk after dinner."). The word *down* can be an adverb ("I fell down when the ball hit me."), a preposition ("Let's walk down the street."), or even a verb ("I downed the Pepsi because I was thirsty.").

Differences in culture can be seen in the use of vocabulary items. For example, the Eskimos have nine different vocabulary items, each of which we would translate into English as "snow." In their language the Eskimos use different words to convey an essentially different aspect of a form of "snow" as it relates to its texture, content, or purpose.

It is very difficult to arrive at a one-for-one equivalent translation for an item in another language. For example, when asked to translate the concept of a "blue-chip company" (that is, a business that has a very high commercial rating) a Hungarian translator used the equivalent phrase in Hungarian for a "company that makes blue chips"—a literal translation, but one that does not convey the meaning of the phrase in English.

ACTIVE VS. PASSIVE VOCABULARY

In some ways, learning new vocabulary is for you a bit like the problem our cavemen heroes faced. At some point you come across a word in a text that you don't recognize; or you hear someone use a word in a conversation that you don't understand; or you want to express an idea but you lack a key word. The problem is, how do you make this vocabulary item a familiar one?

The linguist Mario Pei states that fluency in a language requires a base of 30,000 words, while 10,000 words are the minimum necessary to converse intelligently in another language.

We can begin by distinguishing between *active* and *passive* vocabulary. Simply defined, passive vocabulary is the list of all the words we recognize and understand when we hear or read them. Active vocabulary, on the other hand, consists of those words we use readily and comfortably in our speech and writing. Generally our passive vocabulary word bank is significantly larger than our active vocabulary word bank. That is, we recognize and understand more words that we hear and read than we use ourselves in speech or writing.

Linguists speak of languages as living organisms that are subject to change and growth as they are used by their speakers. (Indeed, Latin and Ancient Greek are considered "dead" languages, frozen in their ancient shapes, because they are no longer spoken.) Of the various subsystems that constitute language—i.e., phonology, morphology, syntax, and semantics—it is the latter subsystem, semantics, which is the most vibrant, the most subject to change. Consider the number of words that have entered into our own language in the last twenty years as a result of technology, historical events, and cultural transference (microchip, détente, glasnost, meltdown, moon walk, rapping).

In considering the full stock of vocabulary items that make up the semantic system of a language, we can make the distinction between *formal* and *informal* language. Simply speaking, formal language is the language of literature, of newspapers, of polite conversation, and writing. Informal language is generally part of spoken language. It will not adhere to all the prescribed rules of phonology, morphology, or syntax. For example, among ourselves in the right situation, the jumble of sounds "Whadyeatin'?" **/wəjiytin/** makes perfect sense and, in fact, may even seem more normal than the perfectly enunciated equivalent "What are you eating?" **/wətaryuwiytiŋ**, even though the first phrase contains fewer sounds and has dropped the auxiliary verb *are*. Informal language may contain grammatical forms that are not allowed in formal language (e.g., I *be* cold. Drive *slow*. He *ain't* heavy.) In terms of semantics, all languages contain *slang*, which consists of vocabulary items that either

1. do not occur in formal language and may not even be found in a dictionary, or
2. have a different use or meaning from the same word's original (i.e., as used in formal language) meaning. (For example, "bad" can mean "good, great, wonderful"; "cool" may mean "wonderful"; "far out" may mean "fantastic".)

You may be surprised at the large number of cognates (words that share the same etymology and that have the same meaning in different languages) you will encounter in learning other languages. For example:

French	Spanish	Italian
art	arte	arte
association	asociación	associazione
comprendre	comprender	comprendere
difficulté	dificultad	difficoltà
honneur	honor	onore
partie	parte	parte
possible	posible	possibile

These items are easier to recognize when written but they may be pronounced very differently (remember that we said there is often a big difference between spelling and pronunciation).

TYPES OF VOCABULARY EXERCISES

1. Reorganize the following groups of letters into words:

[German]   braeit / khspiy / eiielvw
[French]   vleri / éeloc / imnoas
[Italian]   uacsol / cnchaami / aeorrtp

This type of exercise requires recognition of vocabulary items, which may be in conjugated forms, and your task will be easier if you can recognize letter groupings that are possible and eliminate those that don't occur in the target language.

2. "Odd-Man-Out." Choose the word in each group which does not belong:

[German]   Herbst, Frühling, Juli, Sommer
[Spanish] gordo, gato, graso, grande
[French]   salon, cuisine, chambre, garage

With this type of exercise you will need to determine the feature that three of the four words have in common or the category to which they belong in order to figure out why the fourth word doesn't fit. For example, in the Spanish exercise three of the four choices are adjectives that could be used to describe the "odd-man-out" noun, **gato**.

3. Rewrite the following sentences using the opposite of the underlined word:

[Spanish] Pedro es muy <u>serio</u>.
[French] Ce devoir est extremement <u>difficile</u>!
[German] Das Mädchen hat ein <u>klein</u> Buch.
[Italian] Ho visto un cane tutto <u>nero</u>.

In addition to knowing, as part of your active vocabulary word bank, the antonym of the underlined word, you must make sure that you use the correct form. That is, the adjective must agree with the noun in gender and number; a verb must agree with the subject in person and number.

4. Multiple Choice. Choose the word that best completes the meaning of the sentence:

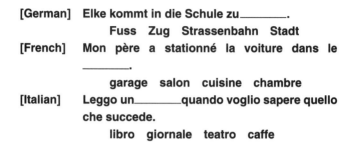

[German]   Elke kommt in die Schule zu_____.
           Fuss   Zug   Strassenbahn   Stadt
[French]   Mon père a stationné la voiture dans le
           _____.
           garage   salon   cuisine   chambre
[Italian] Leggo un_____quando voglio sapere quello
           che succede.
           libro   giornale   teatro   caffe

For this type of exercise you should first read the entire sentence and make sure you understand it. If you do, you can probably figure out what goes into the blank without looking at the possible answers. Try that first, making an intelligent guess and then see if one of the answers matches your guess.

HINTS AND SUGGESTIONS

From the first day, *keep your own lexicon (list of vocabulary items)* in a notebook. Set aside a number of pages in the back of your notebook and try to keep your words in alphabetical order. You might even give a full page to each letter. From time to time, count up the number of words you have learned and keep a tally by date. You will be surprised at how quickly this number increases. Sure, this takes more time. But it is the first step toward building an inventory of active vocabulary items. And writing these items down in your own word bank serves as a method for reinforcing them in your mind. Furthermore, rather than wrestling with a dictionary, which contains thousands of items, you will be working with words you have already studied.

Another effective way of keeping track of vocabulary items is to *group them in your lexicon according to their function*: noun / verb / adjective / adverb / preposition / conjunction. This can be a lot more helpful than a simple alphabetical listing. For example, when you are writing a sentence and know that you need a verb that you have studied but cannot think of the precise word to use, you turn to your list of verbs and look for the right one. You should also alphabetize your nouns, verbs, adjectives, etc., to make them easier for you to find.

Try to learn vocabulary in pairs (e.g., synonyms or antonyms) or groups (related nouns, adjectives, verbs, etc.). For example, you may already know that the French word **heureux** means "happy." Let's use the symbol = to indicate a synonym and the symbol ≠ to indicate an antonym (opposite). When you learn a synonym for **heureux**, which is **content**, and an antonym, **triste**, you should enter them in your lexicon the following way:

content = heureux ≠ triste

Thus, without writing any English translation you have used your knowledge of one word to add two new items to your lexicon. Most important, you are using French to learn more French! Similarly, starting with the word **heureux**, which you already know, you can add three words to your lexicon by showing relationships in the following manner:

| **heureux** | ≠ | **triste** | **(Aj)** |
| **bonheur** | ≠ | **tristesse** | **(Noun)** |

If you want to increase the size of your active vocabulary, or move an item from your passive vocabulary, *use each new word as you learn it*. As in English, using a word gives you control and ownership of it. Then try to use the new word in a meaningful context. For example, use the vocabulary you already know to explain the meaning of new vocabulary items instead of writing the word's meaning in English. (Hopefully, your teacher will also employ this technique, *using* the language to teach more vocabulary.)

When you're faced with learning a long list of vocabulary items (i.e., knowing the translation in the target language for a particular English word and vice versa), *use index cards*. Write the target language word on one side and the English translation on the other. Then form a "deck" of the index cards with all the English facing one direction, the target language words facing the other. Next, move through the deck, looking at the English words and checking to see if you know the corresponding word in the foreign language. Then, begin with the target language side and check to see if you know the English equivalent. As you shuffle through the deck of index cards, you'll gradually be able to look at only one side of the card and say to yourself what appears on the other.

When learning new vocabulary items try to organize them into whatever groups are meaningful to you. *Pictures are helpful memory devices.* For example, a picture of a person with arrows connecting the vocabulary items and parts of the body; or a picture of a house with suitable vocabulary items; or a family tree to indicate the names for various relationships.

Words that can be grouped together because they bear some relationship to one another are *best learned in groups*. For example, the days of the week, months of the year, ordinal numbers, seasons. Or, for example:

always, often, occasionally, sometimes, never
and
yesterday, today, tomorrow

Use mnemonic (memory-aiding) devices to remember words that go together. For example, the "motion" verbs in French that use the auxiliary verb **être** to form compound tenses can be remembered by the mnemonic device **DR&MRSVANDERTAMP**, where each letter represents the first letter of a "motion" verb:

D: descendre	**V: venir**	**R: retourner**
R: revenir	**A: arriver**	**T: tomber**
M: monter	**N: naître**	**A: aller**
R: rentrer	**D: devenir**	**M: mourir**
S: sortir	**E: entrer**	**P: partir**

This same group of verbs can also be represented on a picture, with different indications of the verb actions.

Master the roots in the target language. The roots carry the meaning and will help you decipher related words that contain the same root. (For example, in Arabic, the radical (root) consonants **KTB** carry the base idea of writing, so

KᵃTiB:	"clerk"	**yᵃKTuBu:**	"he writes"
mᵃKTüB:	"document"	**mᵃKTᵃB:**	"office"

Mastery of vocabulary requires a *constant review* (through reading and listening comprehension) and use (through speaking and writing). Your constant goal should be to increase the size of your active and passive vocabulary.

Learn idiomatic expressions as early as you can. An *idiomatic expression* is a group of two or more words whose collective meaning cannot be readily deduced from the meanings of the words in the expression. Idiomatic expressions often give us some insight as to how cultures view the world differently. Compare for example:

[English]	It's all Greek to me.
[French]	Pour moi c'est de l'hébreu.
	"For me it's Hebrew."
[German]	Das sind böhmische Dörfer für mich.
	"It's Bohemian villages to me."
[Spanish]	Para mí eso es griego o gringo.
	"For me it's Greek or jibberish."

Idiomatic expressions may seem extremely logical or illogical. (English speakers have little problem with French **J'*ai* mal à la tête**, "I have a headache," but sometimes can't understand why the French use the same verb to express "I'm hungry," **J'*ai* faim**.)

Finally, *do not rely too heavily on a dictionary.* The temptation is to think that a dictionary will solve any problems we have when we hear, read, or have to speak or write using an unfamiliar vocabulary item. Americans sometimes have the mistaken notion that, armed with the right dictionary, they can master any foreign language. Remember that a language is much more than a random collection of words.

SEVEN

LEARNING TO READ A FOREIGN LANGUAGE

The linguistic skill of learning to read a language, whether a foreign language or your native tongue, involves being able to decode the meaningful units on a page of print or on a sign. You will read in the target language for the same reasons you read in English, that is, for information and enjoyment. You read in different ways (i.e., quickly by scanning or carefully, word by word) depending on why you are reading and the nature of what you are reading. For example, in the foreign language classroom you will have occasion to read: dialogues, captions under pictures, short reading selections, lists of vocabulary items, short stories, plays, and novels.

Reading is not a totally passive activity because it requires that the reader become engaged in the process of decoding the writer's message. In terms of involvement on the part of the reader we can distinguish between *intensive* and *extensive* reading. Intensive reading is done for accuracy, under the guidance of a teacher, answering questions about information contained in the reading selection and even explicating the author's style. Extensive reading is done for fluency, for entertainment, and/or for increasing vocabulary.

Reading will also unlock clues as to the culture and customs of those who use the target language.

There are various reasons why a French I student who has just finished the English translation of Camus's *L'Étranger* cannot just pick up a copy of the original and read it. Primarily he lacks the vocabulary and knowledge of grammar to decode the words on the page and arrange them into ideas. Even a student at an advanced level would have to have an understanding of Franco-Algerian society as well as of Camus's philosophy to appreciate the novel fully.

Learning to read a foreign language is a gradual process. Think back to when you were just starting to read English. You started with words you recognized alone and then learned to decipher them in phrases and sentences. Learning to read a foreign language will entail some of the same steps, although will move along at a quicker pace because you already are familiar with the reading process itself.

Learning to read a language that does not use a Latin alphabet will first entail learning to recognize and differentiate the various *graphemes* (i.e., "letters"). You will be required to "sound out" the words you read to prove that you have recognized them correctly. A list of familiar items (such as the names of the fifty United States) written using the symbols of the target language alphabet can be a helpful learning device.

Initial exposure to reading in a foreign language class usually occurs in conjunction with a dialogue that is practiced over and over for speaking and pronunciation. Reading selections at the beginning level of a language will reinforce vocabulary you encounter by rearranging it in a different meaningful setting. New vocabulary will then be added to the old in the assumption that you can figure out its meaning from the context. Usually a translation of the meaning of each new vocabulary item or phrase will be found next to or after the reading selection, but you should try to figure out what they mean before consulting the glossary.

Your first experience with reading the target language will come when your teacher requires you to read aloud written sentences and passages. This experience can be very threatening. Your teacher will want you to read sentences or dialogues aloud to check on your pronunciation and intonation and also to see if you have a sense for what you are reading, if you can group ideas together. For example, if you pause in the middle of a noun phrase or separate a preposition from the noun phrase it introduces, or a subject from a verb, this may signal that you don't understand what you are reading.

The next step (before free reading) will be reading pictorial magazines (such as *Paris Match*, *Star*, *Ora*) and comic books (such as *Asterix*). You're not going to be able to understand everything that you read at first, so you should look for visual clues to help you understand what the unfamiliar vocabulary may mean. You should also use logic. For example, let's say you're reading a sequence of actions and you encounter a verb which you don't recognize; ask yourself what action might logically follow the others.

Learning to read for comprehension in a foreign language means being able to understand what is written *in that language* without the intermediary step of translating it first into English. Thus, your goal is to understand (i.e., form a mental picture of) the ideas that are presented in the foreign language. If you can understand a word, phrase, or sentence in a foreign language, you don't need to translate it (probably poorly) into English. And learning to read for comprehension entails moving from words to phrases to sentences *in the target language* without having to translate first into English.

When reading a novel for comprehension and later discussion use marks in the margins (stars, checks, vertical lines) to signal those sentences you think are significant to the development or interpretation of the story. Underline or circle powerful descriptive words or phrases. At the same time keep a log of vocabulary items that are new or unfamiliar to you.

READING COMPREHENSION EXERCISES

Questions, either oral or written, or multiple-choice selections are usually used to test reading comprehension. The questions may be rather general or very specific.

Typically, in your first-year language class you will encounter specific (who/what/when/where/which/how/yes/no) questions that test your ability to absorb specific information from a reading selection or dialogue as well as to express it in clear, grammatically correct sentences. For example, after reading a dialogue you might encounter the following exercise:

1. Determine if the following statements are true or false. If the statement is true write **Richtig**; if it is false, write **Falsch** and correct the sentence so that it is true.

> **Elke findet einen Pulli schick.**
> **Richtig.**
> **Sie hat nur ein paar Pullis.**
> **Falsch. Sie hat viele Pullis.**

Or, for example, after reading a selection about a couple of students you might be asked questions such as:

> [German] **Wer geht in die Schule zu Fuss?**
> [French] **Comment Marie arrive-t-elle à l'école?**
> [Italian] **Maria viene alla scuola nella machina?**
> [Spanish] **¿Donde va María después de las tres?**

For both these types of exercise you will need to identify the specific information—i.e., who/what/when/where/which or whether the statement or question is true or false—that is requested and then refer back to the sentence(s) that contains that information. In answering a question you should use the words and structure of the question, replacing the specific question word with your specific answer. For example, in the French example, **Comment**, "How?" is specifically answered by **à pied**, "on foot," and the word order of the question is changed into the word order for a statement to produce the answer.

Marie arrive à l'école à pied.

2. Slightly more sophisticated questions will require you to deduce new information from what is contained in the reading selection. For example, if you read that most students in Germany take public transportation or walk to school, you might be asked (in German): Do most American students travel to school the way German students do?

3. As you progress in the target language you will be asked to give explications of sentences or passages. For example, you may be asked to explain the significance of a pair of sentences drawn from a novel. In order to do an acceptable explication you need to:

- indicate the action and setting (i.e., who/when/where);
- explain how this passage relates to the rest of the story;
- point out the importance of the author's choice of words;
- explain what the passage reveals about a character.

For example, in Camus's *L'Étranger* we find the sentence:

J'ai eu un moment l'impression ridicule qu'ils étaient là pour me juger.
(For a moment I had the silly feeling that they were there to judge me.)

You would be expected to indicate that **J(e)** refers to the narrator, Meursault; that **ils** ("they") are the friends of his mother who have come to her wake; that the narrator has this feeling on the night before his mother's funeral at the old folks' home where she had been living; that this isn't the first time that others are judging him.

HINTS AND SUGGESTIONS

Here follow some hints for learning how to read a foreign language:

When you are just beginning to learn a foreign language and have a series of sentences to read, *break the sentence down into each of its elements*, using brackets or lines to separate the parts or phrases of larger sentences. You might even try to identify and label the various elements (i.e., subject/verb/direct object, etc.) of each sentence. For example, faced with the sentence:

Le petit garçon a trouvé le livre dans le salon.

you would break it into the following components:

S	V	DO	Av
(Le petit garçon)	(a trouvé)	(le livre)	(dans le salon.)

At an intermediate level (that is, before you start reading novels and plays) you may be drawn to magazines or comic books. Look at the pictures for clues to help you decipher the meanings of words you don't know. The combination of words you understand and the visual clues provided by the picture will often be enough to help you figure out the meaning of the new word. (And now you can add another entry to your passive vocabulary word bank.) Advertisements for familiar products will also give you lots of clues as to the meaning of unfamiliar words.

HIGHER-LEVEL READING

What follows is a system for reading at a more advanced level. It is predicated on the use of a dictionary as a last resort for determining the meaning of a word that is unfamiliar.

When you are faced with the task of longer reading passages, *first scan the entire reading selection* to get a general idea of what the paragraph or short selection is about. Don't worry about words that you don't know. On the second reading *underline words that you don't know.*

When faced with a vocabulary item you are unable to decode, *check the stem of the word for a clue.* Does it look like another word you have learned? For example, in the following sentences in Spanish, you might not know the meaning of the word **bebida**:

> **Mucha gente dice que el chocolate era la bebida favorita del emperador Moctezuma. Pero el chocolate que Moctezuma bebía no tenía azúcar.**

You might deduce that **bebida** is related to a word which you already know, the verb **bebía** (from **beber**, "to drink") in the following sentence. Because of the context "la_____favorita," you know that **bebida** must be a noun, so you deduce it means "(a) drink."

Try to *figure out the meaning* of the underlined words *from the context.* If you are really stuck, you might first replace the word you don't know with a blank (_____) to determine what part of speech (noun/verb/adjective/adverb/preposition/conjunction) it is. For example, in reading the following short paragraph in Ital-

75

ian about a boy going back to school after summer vacation you are not sure of the meaning of the word **brulicavano**:

> **Tutte le strade brulicavano di ragazzi; le due botteghe di libraio erano affollate di padri e di madri che compravano zaini, cartelle e quaderni. . . .**

By examining the rest of the context you might deduce the following:

1. **brulicavano** is a verb; you know this from the fact that if you replaced it with a blank: **Tutte le strade _____di ragazzi**, you would see that there is no verb in the sentence. If your grammar is up to snuff, you could tell from the ending of **brulicavano** that it is third-person, plural imperfect tense of the infinitive **brulicare**.

2. The rest of the sentence talks about "stores being mobbed" with people buying things.

3. So, you might hazard a guess that **brulicavano** might mean something like "were teeming, packed (with)."

When you have tried these other measures, *use the dictionary to confirm what you have been able to figure out* with your knowledge of the language. In the previous case, you would verify that **brulicare** means "to swarm."

Of course there will be times when a dictionary will be the most expeditious way to determine a word's meaning. The problem is that if you become too dependent on a dictionary, if you resort to using a dictionary every time you run into a word you don't recognize immediately, you risk dulling the skills you have been honing.

Remember that in chapter 6 we indicated that words can have more than a single meaning, depending on their context. In looking for the meaning of a word in a dictionary you must first do some preliminary detective work. For example, with verbs you must first determine the stem or the infinitive form.

It is important to read the entire entry in the dictionary, especially when the vocabulary item has more than a single meaning or may be different parts of speech.

Simplify long complex sentences by *reducing complex sentences to their bare essentials* (i.e., "Who does/did what?"). You can do this by identifying first the verb, then the subject of the verb (i.e., "who?"), and then what the verb introduces.

In complex, multi-proposition sentences look for clue connecting words that help relate one part of the sentence to another. For example, the following conjunctions serve to relate information in proposition #1 with information in proposition #2:

Proposition #1	Conjunction	Proposition #2
	and	
	but	
	therefore	
	because	
	although	
	when	
	in order that	

If you understand the meaning of the conjunction, then you can deduce the relationship between the two propositions, and understanding of the meaning of the contents of one of the propositions will enable you to figure out the general meaning of the other proposition.

Make reading into an interactive skill by *formulating questions* about what you have been reading and making sure that you can answer the questions yourself. (Since answering questions is a normal learning activity in a foreign language class, you could suggest to your teacher that the students be allowed to prepare the questions.) As your knowledge of the target language increases your questions will change from information seeking (yes/no/who/what/where/when) to interpretive (how/why).

EIGHT

LEARNING TO WRITE A FOREIGN LANGUAGE

The active linguistic skill of writing in a foreign language involves encoding, that is, translating ideas into grammatically correct structures, using appropriate vocabulary, and spelling correctly.

For languages that do not use the Latin alphabet (such as Greek, Russian, Arabic, or Chinese), your first step in learning to write the target language will entail learning to form the *graphemes*, or written symbols of the language. Even with languages that use the Latin alphabet (such as French, German, Italian, Turkish), you will have to familiarize yourself with the use of accents and diacritical marks that are used to signal differences in pronunciation. (For example, in French **é** and **è** are pronounced differently from one another and from the unaccented **e**. In German, **ü** is pronounced differently from **u**.)

A difference in pronunciation that signals a difference in meaning may be reflected in the writing system. For example, in German the ¨ over a vowel (called an "umlaut") signals the meaning of "plural": **Apfel** ("apple"), **Äpfel** ("apples"); **Vater** ("father"), **Väter** ("fathers"); **Bruder** ("brother"), **Brüder** ("brothers"); **Tochter** ("daughter"), **Töchter** ("daughters"); **Mutter** ("mother"), **Mütter** ("mothers").

Your first experience with writing in a foreign language, as with speaking, will be very structured. (You will not be expected to produce a novel or even to tell what you did over your summer vacation. Your teacher will restrict your writing assignments to what you can handle.) You will probably begin by writing or copying short sentences from material you are studying orally. Then you will move on to answering specific questions about a dialogue you have been practicing or a reading selection.

The purpose of these questions is to determine whether you have understood the content of the dialogue or reading selection, whether you can use the new vocabulary you have encountered, and whether you can restate the information you have absorbed in new, grammatically correct sentences. Remember that the difference between writing and simply copying written information (as you did when you were first learning to write in English) is that you are manipulating the vocabulary and grammatical structures of the foreign languages to create sentences that are *new for you*. That is why writing is an active *creative* linguistic skill.

Again, the first types of questions you will be asked to answer will be very structured. (They will not be analytical, psychological, or philosophical, such as "What is your opinion as to why the hero decided to foresake his love in order to avenge his father's honor?" We'll save that sort of question for a fifth-year discussion of *Le Cid*.) You will be asked to respond to two types of questions:

1. questions that require a "yes" or "no" response;
2. questions that require a specific answer and begin with a specific interrogative word (who/what/when/where/why/how?)

You may be wondering how to distinguish between these two types of questions. The yes/no question may differ from a statement only because the question is accompanied by a question mark (**?**) at the end of the sentence (or, in the case of Spanish a **¿** at the beginning of the sentence and a **?** at the end). The word order may be the same as that used in a statement. For example:

[German]	Hans sprecht Deutsch?
[Italian]	Luigi parla italiano?
[French]	Marc parle français?
[Spanish]	¿José habla español?

In French a yes/no question may also be signaled by the marker **Est-ce que**, which is placed at the beginning of the sentence (e.g., **Est-ce que Louis parle français?**). **Est-ce que** has no real "translation" but merely signals that a question is occurring; in some ways it serves the same function as the **¿** written at the beginning of a Spanish question. However, **Est-ce que** also occurs in speech and is not just a written marker.

Languages may also use *inversion* to signal a question. This means that the word order used in a statement of subject + verb is reversed, that is, the subject comes after the verb in a question. (In English we also use inversion in a question: "Are you all right?" "Do you have any money?") For example:

[German]	Haben Sie Geld?
[French]	Avez-vous de l'argent?
[Spanish]	¿Tiene usted dinero?

Remember from chapter 5 that written language tends to be more formal (i.e., grammatically correct) than spoken language. In a written French question, if the subject is a noun phrase the pronoun equivalent of the subject noun phrase is used in inversion. For example,

Le nouveau maire aime-t-il son bureau?

(This type of inversion would not occur in speech.)

No matter how the yes/no question is signaled, your task is a relatively simple one—namely, to determine whether the information in the question is true or false. If it is true you will begin your written answer with the equivalent of "yes"; if the information is false you will begin your answer with the equivalent of "no." Then, all you have to do is repeat the core information provided in the question. For example,

Hans geht nach München? Ja, Hans geht nach München.

As you become more comfortable with the language you'll substitute a pronoun for **Hans** and an adverb for **nach München.**

Ja, er geht da.

The second type of question you will be asked to answer contains a specific interrogative word (i.e., the equivalent of who/what/when/where):

[Italian] *Dove* va Maria?
[French] *Quand* arrive le train?
[German] *Wen* fragt Frau Müller?
[Spanish] *¿Quién* tiene el dinero?

Answering specific questions is a bit more complex but can be made easier if you follow this suggestion. First of all, separate the specific interrogative word from the rest of the sentence:

Dove // va Maria?

to determine what exactly is being looked for in the way of an answer. Analyze the main part of the question (i.e., **va** is the verb; **Maria** is the subject). (In fact the subject of the verb follows the verb in the first three examples above. This may take some getting used to for a speaker of English.) **Dove** means "where?" So you are being asked: "Where is Maria going?" Find the answer to **Dove** (let's say it's **alla scuola**, "to school") and tack it onto the main part of the question, using the order for a statement. Thus,_____**va Maria?** Becomes **Maria va**_____, to which you add **alla scuola** to construct the answer statement **Maria va alla scuola**.

It is important to understand the grammatical role of the question word and the other parts of the sentence in order to determine the meaning of the question and, thus, the correct response. For example, German makes the distinction between the subject form **Wer** ("Who?") and the object form **Wen** ("Whom?"), which we speakers of English may use in writing but rarely use in speech. Thus, the two German questions

Wer seht Frau Müller?
Wen seht Frau Müller?

are syntactically different. In the first sentence **Frau Müller** is the direct object of the verb **seht** because **Wer** can only be a subject; in the second sentence **Frau Müller** is the subject of **seht** because **Wen** can only be an object. Know your grammar!

CONTROLLED COMPOSITION

Controlled composition is an intermediary step between answering structured questions and free writing in the process of learning to write in a foreign language. The goal of controlled composition is to get you to practice using grammatical structures and to understand how vocabulary can be interrelated grammatically, while you are becoming more at ease with writing. Typically, a controlled composition exercise will involve making a number of changes while rewriting a paragraph or two. It is up to you to determine which words must be changed and how they must be rewritten. For example, the following short paragraph is about an Italian boy who is studying English because he wants to become a pilot.

> Luigi è uno studente italiano di sedici anni che abita un piccolo villagio vicino a Firenze. Suo fratello è pilote per l'Alitalia. Alla scuola Luigi studia l'inglese perché vuole divenire pilote. Lui sa che deve sapere bene questa lingua.

A typical controlled composition exercise might require you to change **Luigi** to **Maria e Francesca** or might ask you to change the verbs to the past tense or both. (The words you need to change may or may not be underlined.)

EXPANDING IDEAS

At first your writing will be rather simple and "unsophisticated," consisting of short sentences that may be little more than

Subject	+	Verb	+	Object/Complement
Maria		vede		l'uccello.
Le héros		prend		son épée.
Der Zug		kommt		im Bahnhof.
El gato		es		muy gordo.

This may cause you a bit of frustration; after all, you are older but you are producing sentences that are at the level of what you were writing in first or second grade. You need to understand a bit about the grammar of the language you are studying in order to "flesh out" your simple sentences. (It will take lots of time and practice to arrive at sentences that are as grammatically complex as you now write in English, but you will be surprised at how quickly this will come.) For example, a simple noun phrase (determiner + noun) such as **le héros** can be expanded by the addition of adjectives, an appositive noun phrase, a prepositional phrase, or a relative clause:

> le héros
> le brave et noble héros de ce roman
> le héros, un guerrier brave et noble
> le héros qui venge son père.

WRITING EXERCISES

For languages that are not usually written in the Latin alphabet, you may be asked to transpose words from script to their Latin alphabet equivalent. In order to perform this type of exercise successfully, you must learn how to recognize and form the various graphemes and to "translate" them into their equivalent spellings in the Latin alphabet. Success in this area, unfortunately, may depend more on brute memorization. However, there are some "memory aids" for each language that your teacher will point out to you.

1. Rearrange the following letters to form nouns:

[French]	TEVUORI, OMISAN, AERMHCB
[German]	BTRAIE, MMYNUIGSA, HELRRE
[Italian]	FOPERSEOS, LOAUSC, AANCTER

This type of exercise is often used at the very beginning level to see if you remember vocabulary you have been learning. It is helpful in unscrambling letters to know which letter combinations are possible.

2. Rearrange the following words to form complete sentences:

[German]   nicht / ins / darf / fahren / heute / ich / Kino / abend.

[French]   rend / ses / professeur / devoirs / les / le / à / élèves

[Spanish]   devuelve / estudiantes / tarea / el / a / les / los / la / profesor

[Italian]   ragazzo / trovare / il / madre / non / sua / può / piccolo

This exercise can be fun because it requires you to do a bit of detective work. First, you need to determine the main verb, which is the nucleus of the sentence; then you find the noun, pronoun, or noun phrase that is the subject of the verb. How do you figure this out? Well, does the verb's ending give you a clue? Next, ask yourself whether the verb takes a direct object, indirect object, neither, or both. Make sure that determiners and adjectives agree with whatever nouns you place them with. For example, in the French sentence, the verb **rend** is third-person singular, so the only one of the three nouns that could be its subject is **professeur**. The verb **rend** can take both a direct object (a thing), **devoirs**, and an indirect object (a person, here introduced by the preposition **à**), **élèves**.

One of the exercises you will encounter in language class, particularly at the elementary level, will be **dictations**. These exercises are useful to check your ability to spell in the foreign language and to comprehend what you are hearing by being able to "translate" the spoken stream of speech into separate written words. Another form of dictation exercises, particularly with rapidly spoken material or with songs, are cloze passages in which most of the spoken material is written down for you and you are expected to fill in the blanks with words you hear.

As you begin reading enrichment material that is increasingly sophisticated (in terms of vocabulary and grammatical structures), your teacher is bound to ask you to rewrite in your own words in the foreign language a **précis** or

summary of what the reading selection is all about. The operative phrase here is "in your own words." Ideally, the teacher expects you to be able to absorb the reading material, close the book, and render an accurate (in terms of vocabulary and grammar) account of what you have just read.

Your reaction to such an assignment may naturally be one of awe and fear: "How can I possibly be expected to write as well as_____? After all, he/she is a famous writer. I'm just a struggling language student!" But, don't despair. You're not being asked to reproduce *Don Quixote* or *L'Étranger*, just an accurate explanation of important aspects of the plot.

HINTS AND SUGGESTIONS

Get a pen pal. Write to that person frequently (at least once a week. If you wait for a response to your letter each time, the month the mails take for your letter to get there and a response to come back will discourage you). Write in the target language. If your school has access to Internet correspond with a student at another school via electronic mail. Treat your pen pal as a friend, telling him/her about yourself, your family and friends, what you do at school and on weekends. Here's a chance to use the target language, employing practical vocabulary to convey information.

The following hints are applicable to writing at an intermediate to advanced level, as you begin to move away from answers to specific questions and approach free writing.

Try to rewrite in your own words what you have been reading about. The vocabulary and structures will then be familiar. A certain amount of "translating" will occur naturally until you become fluent in the foreign language. But first identify the main ideas you are trying to convey with the correct vocabulary items in the foreign language. *Consult your own lexicon* (as was discussed in chapter 6) *and the vocabulary lists* that accompany the reading selection. Use a dictionary only after these other resources.

Keep your writing simple. Avoid trying to reproduce the linguistically complex sentences that you are capable of writing in English. Stick with the vocabulary and grammatical structures you have already learned. They will always be sufficient for any assignment you are given. When first beginning to write in the foreign language you might even try sketching out the skeleton for each sentence using "key words," then putting the skin on the bones. For example,

garçon   / aller   / école

expands to:

Le petit garçon   est allé   à l'école.

Keep your story in the same time frame. For example, if you are retelling an event that took place in the past, use only past tenses; do not drift into the present or future tense. Decide before you begin writing whether you will be telling your story from a présent or past **point of view** and stick to that point of view. You need to be aware that, depending on your point of view, you are limited to the tenses you can use. For example, if you are telling a story from the present point of view you will use one set of tenses (i.e., the *present* for current actions; the *past* for what has been completed; the *future* for what is to come). However, if you choose to tell a story from the past point of view, you must use a different set of tenses. For example, in English from the present point of view:

Marie **says** that she **has seen** the movie and **will write** a review. This can be depicted on a time-frame chart:

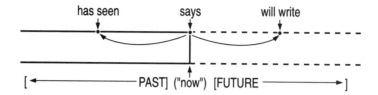

while from a past point of view, the sentence would be:

Marie **said** that she **had seen** the movie and **would write** a review. This can be depicted on a time-frame chart:

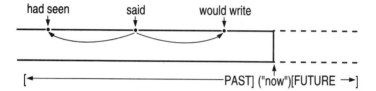

Never *write a composition first in English* and then try to translate it into the foreign language. The temptation here is that you will try to look up all the words that you don't know in the dictionary. However, you will soon discover that your knowledge of English will always be too advanced for what you have learned in the foreign language and you will only be frustrated. The result of this approach is usually a lot of jibberish.

When you must look up a word in a dictionary, be sure that you *use a bilingual* (e.g., French-English/English-French) *dictionary*. The reason is that you may look for a word, find several translations, and not know which one to use. For example, you're writing a composition about a World War II battle and you want to find the French word for "tank." You go to your dictionary and you find that you can choose from **réservoir, citerne, char**. If you picked the second choice and wrote that the German **citernes** were faster and more lethal than the French **citernes**, you would be talking about a battle of large water containers. However, if you had a bilingual dictionary you could check the English translations for the various choices and determine that the only correct word is **char**.

Before you begin writing a composition take the time to *sketch an outline*, noting key vocabulary items, themes, ideas.

Write the rough drafts of a composition *on every other line*. This will leave room for your corrections on the line above. For example,

(corrections)	*élèves sont entrés dans*
(original line with teacher's marks)	*Les élèves ont entré la salle de classe*

If you are unsure of the spelling of a vocabulary item, check in the dictionary. However, let's say you are taking a test and are not given access to a dictionary. Close your eyes and try visualizing how the word should appear on a piece of paper. Then try writing the item in the margin and see if it looks right. If you're unsure of two or three possibilities, write them all out and see which looks best.

NINE

LANGUAGE AND CULTURE

According to the linguist Benjamin Whorf's theory of *linguistic relativity,* the language an individual speaks determines the way in which that person experiences the world in which he/she lives. Simply speaking, we can only relate our experiences in terms of the vocabulary items and grammatical features available to us in our own language. (You may even come across terms from another language that are used by speakers of English because they feel that these foreign terms more closely translate what they want to say.)

Earlier we cited the example of the Eskimo who uses nine different words in his language for what a speaker of English would always call "snow." The Eskimo makes more semantic distinctions because these differences are more important to the Eskimo's culture than they are to the speaker of English. Likewise, you can imagine that the language of a tribe inhabiting the dense tropical jungle might not even contain a word for "snow."

Culture is defined by *The American Heritage Dictionary* as "the totality of socially transmitted behavior patterns, arts, beliefs, institutions, and all other products of human work and thought characteristic of a community or population." Any language is both an aspect of culture (because language is a socially transmitted behavior) and a means for transmitting the behavior patterns and thoughts which constitute culture.

The linguist Robert Lado writes in his book *Linguistics through Cultures* that cultures are "structured systems of patterned behavior." The culture of a particular ethnic group consists of the collection of beliefs and actions that constitute for that people the experience we call life. If asked to define or explain what their culture is made up of, the French, the Spanish, or the Germans (or our fellow Americans) would probably give a list of things they do or believe that makes them different from people of other cultures.

So maybe we should focus on some of the aspects of other cultures which are different from what we do or believe in America. But a caveat here! Remember back in chapter 6 when we asked the question of which word is "correct"—**dog, cane, Hund,** or **chien**? We answered that there is no one single "correct" word for anything in nature because there is no necessary relationship between language and the things language represents. Similarly, there is no one necessarily correct set of customs. If you ask members of another culture why they

eat a particular food at a certain time of day
wear a certain article of clothing
celebrate a particular religious feast

you may receive a reaction of wonderment—What a silly question! Why are you asking it?—or the answer may be "Because it's our way." Do *you* know why you eat cereal or bacon and eggs at breakfast; why you wear white socks when you play sports; why kids dress up in costumes and go trick-or-treating on Halloween? Or are these actions just habits, what we do in the United States?

There is certainly a great deal of linguistic and cultural borrowing among the nations of the world. French and Italian fashions always seem to be in vogue in the United States; everywhere else Levi's and Timberland shoes are the rage. Cuisines considered "exotic" in the United States twenty years ago have become quite popular—witness the number of Korean, Thai, Vietnamese and Indian restaurants. We speak of eating a "Continental" breakfast when we eat a light meal or refer to a late dinner as "very European." A number of vocabulary items have passed directly into English from other languages, virtually unchanged because they have no exact equivalent in English:

[French] avant-garde, coup d'état, déjà vu, détente, faux pas, fait accompli, joie de vivre, laissez-faire
[German] autobahn, ersatz, gesundheit, torte, verboten, wanderlust
[Spanish] aficionado, bonanza, corrida, junta, tortilla

Hopefully, you will have the opportunity to visit a country where the language you are studying is spoken and to experience firsthand the culture of that people. The best advice you can receive in that regard is to keep your eyes and ears open and to withhold judgment. There is no necessarily better way of doing things, just different ways that may be more suited to different cultures. After all, different peoples have had generations or centuries to modify and refine their customs and daily routines.

Another warning. Don't assume that a single experience with a few members of a culture is true for all members of that culture. Old episodes of "Dallas" are shown on European television. Many Europeans who have not had much contact with Americans assume that Americans are like the characters on "Dallas," or that Americans live like the characters on "Dynasty."

Do you think that this is an accurate description of Americans and American culture? Of course not.

Yet, you may hear an American say "I hate the French" and when you ask why, you'll hear that on his trip to Paris last August (when most Parisians have fled the city), the waiters in a restaurant were rude, refusing to understand his English. Basing a disregard for all Frenchmen on this experience is about as fair as a Frenchman condemning all Americans because of his first encounters with an unfriendly cab driver or waiter in New York City.

Preconceived notions about a people, such as

All Germans love beer
The Dutch all wear wooden shoes
Every Japanese is small
All Arab women cover their faces

will only create a serious obstacle to learning about that culture. Don't create stereotypes in your mind. You are an individual; so are your counterparts in other cultures.

CULTURAL DIFFERENCES

Perhaps some examples of practices or behaviors in other cultures that are different from what we are used to as Americans will be helpful.

Many Europeans prefer to do their shopping for food at smaller neighborhood specialty shops (the butcher's, the baker's, the greengrocer's) where meeting other neighbors and chatting with the shop owner is part of the ritual, rather than at a large impersonal supermarket. However, supermarchés (and even larger hypermarchés) can be found on the perimeters of many cities and large towns in western Europe. These hypermarchés offer, in addition to food, automotive and sporting goods, clothing, housewares and gardening supplies, all under one roof.

Shopping may be followed by a stop at a café for an espresso or cappuccino, a glass of beer or wine. Cafés have a life of their own; the clients are not rushed and you can sit with your drink as long as you wish, chatting with a friend, playing cards, reading a newspaper (from the café's newspaper rack), or just watching people walk by. (One of my fondest memories is of playing chess with a student at a St. Moritz corner café while enjoying a cup of cappuccino in the bright January sunshine.)

It is important to note that the glass of beer or wine (just like the cup of coffee or tea) is part of the café or restaurant "ritual." Too many American students on their first trip to Europe seize on the culture's license for them to drink as an opportunity to drink as much as they can. The *quantity* to be consumed becomes their goal and they completely miss the ritual. Not surprisingly, their European counterparts find their behavior immature or a sign of bad upbringing.

The timing and content of meals differ from culture to culture. Only the British eat the very full breakfast, which used to be an American ritual. In many western European countries the largest meal is consumed in the middle of the day.

Rather than gathering around the television to watch a football or baseball game on a Sunday afternoon, many families love to go for a stroll in the park or around town. Italians dress up in their finest for **farsi vedere**.

Many European teenagers don't pair off and "date" as American teenagers do. They're more likely to go out in small groups of friends.

Manners of greeting will vary from culture to culture and will depend on the relationship of the people who are meeting. You may see people kissing one another two or three times on the cheek and men embracing one another. The language may even have different salutations for friends as opposed to acquaintances or strangers. Title and honorifics ("sir, madam") may be expected. French, German, Spanish, and Italian have a different form for "you" depending on whether you are addressing friends, relatives, or strangers.

	informal sing.	formal sing.	informal plural	formal plural
[French]	tu	vous	vous	vous
[German]	du	Sie	ihr	Sie
[Italian]	tu	lei	voi	voi
[Spanish]	tú	usted	vosotros	ustedes

In indicating time the rest of the world uses a twenty-four-hour clock for schedules. For example, if you are in a train station looking for a train that leaves at 1:40 in the afternoon, you should be looking for 13:40 because you will never see the indication "P.M." (or "A.M.").

CULTURAL GAFFES

Loosely defined, a cultural gaffe is a mistake in behavior or language that is made because a person assumes that what works in one culture will automatically work in another.

Here are some examples of cultural gaffes:

- A number of years ago General Motors tried to market its very popular Chevrolet Nova in Latin America but sales were minimal. Company executives didn't realize that **No va** in Spanish means "It doesn't go." Hardly an endorsement for a car.
- When Pepsi's slogan used to be "Come Alive with Pepsi," a poor translation into German gave the equivalent of "Come Alive Out of the Grave with Pepsi." How do you think sales went?

- Equally inept translation rendered "tonic water" as "bathroom water" in Italian and the Schweppes people found that they were having trouble selling their product in Italy.
- Unsuspecting tourists will incur the wrath of pious Muslims by entering a mosque without first removing their shoes.

Cultural gaffes can be avoided by taking the time to understand the language and culture of the target country, and by not assuming that what works in one country will be acceptable in another.

At a time when the United States bemoans the growing trade deficit, the American business community is starting to realize that it takes no knowledge of another language to buy products from another country, but that it takes considerable knowledge of another country's language and culture to market and sell products there. Are we as a nation truly prepared to deal with the emerging united European economic market? Senator Paul Simon reminds us that the United States is the only country in the world where a person can graduate from college without studying another language, while in most other countries students are required to study another language for a number of years *before* entering university.

BODY LANGUAGE

Learning to speak another language will also entail mastery of the body language with which speakers of the target language accompany speech. Body language encompasses such things as gestures, tone, demeanor, and stance. Using proper body language will enhance what you have to say in the target language. Improper body language will not only detract from your message, but it may result in your message being considered not worth hearing.

Aspects of body language will vary from culture to culture and can best be learned by watching and imitating the native speakers of the language. For example, in Japan a man refers to himself by pointing to his nose; a woman does the same by pointing to her chest. In India "yes" is signaled by a head movement that looks a lot to a Westerner like our signal for "no." Waving a hand in front of one's face in Japan can mean "no," "I don't know," or "I don't understand."

In order to learn some of the aspects of body language in another culture you should check the following points:

- How do they greet one another? Is there bowing, hand shaking, kissing?
- What distance do they remain from one another?
- Do they look directly at one another?
- Do they raise their voices to signal emotion or for emphasis?
- What arm motions or hand gestures are used? Are these linked to any specific vocabulary items or phrases for emphasis?

TEN

"YOUR PASSPORT TO THE WORLD": A SUMMING UP

We have examined the various reasons why learning a foreign language makes sense for someone your age who will have increasingly frequent opportunities to come into contact with other languages and cultures and how being fluent in a foreign language will add to your personal portfolio and be your passport to exploring our shrinking world. Language is a skill and a speaker of several languages has a distinct advantage over a speaker of just one language.

We have seen that language is a system composed of various subsystems: *phonology* (the system of sounds), *morphology* (the system of rules for word formation), *syntax* (the system of rules for phrase and sentence construction), and *semantics* (the system of words and meanings). We have also noted that these subsystems operate interdependently and that the rules for any of the subsystems may vary from one language to another. However, it is the essential features all languages share in general that make it possible for us to study and learn another language. It is the features that differ from one language to the next that may pose problems for us in learning another language, especially if we tend to transfer our own language features to the other language.

We noted that fluency in a language, whether our native language or a foreign language, entails mastery of the four linguistic skills of *listening comprehension, speaking, reading,* and *writing.* Listening comprehension and reading are passive skills; speaking and writing are active skills. *Grammar,* though not a linguistic skill, is crucial to the ability to understand and use a language.

Listening comprehension and speaking are aural/oral skills, the mastery of which require the ability to recognize and produce the sounds of the foreign language as well as those sound features that make for differences in meaning (such as pitch, tone, intonation, pause). Mastery also includes the ability to recognize individual words and ideas from the stream of spoken speech, and to communicate ideas by correctly producing the sounds, vocabulary items, and longer phrases and sentences.

In discussing vocabulary we made the distinction between *passive* and *active* vocabulary. Passive vocabulary consists of the bank of words we comprehend when we hear them spoken or when we read them, and this bank is usually significantly larger than the number of words in our active vocabulary, that is, the words we use in speech and writing. We also noted the distinction between formal and informal language, the latter containing slang.

We noted that learning to read in a foreign language involves being able to decode the string of written words in a passage so as to understand the ideas represented. We reviewed strategies for unlocking the meaning of complex sentences, such as using brackets to separate the various components of the sentence and using the context to provide clues for discovering the meaning of an unfamiliar word.

Learning to write in a foreign language, we noted, is a gradual process that, in a foreign language class, typically begins with answering questions about a dialogue or reading selection and later progresses into writing plot synopses. We suggested strategies for answering yes/no and interrogative-word questions as well as for "fleshing out" grammatically simple sentences.

It was noted that the four linguistic skills cannot be studied independently of one another, as they are intrinsically related. We looked at how, in the foreign language classroom, learning activities often pass from a passive skill (listening comprehension or reading) to an active skill (speaking or writing). In the chapters dealing with the four linguistic skills and those dealing with grammar and vocabulary we reviewed types of exercises that will be used to test ability and comprehension and we looked at strategies for successfully "attacking" these exercises.

Finally, we explored the relationship of language and culture, noting that language is both a manifestation of a culture and the primary means for communicating aspects of the culture. We noted that cultural behavior is not intrinsically right or wrong, but is the result of generations, sometimes centuries, of practice and modification. We warned against making preconceptions or accepting stereotypes of members of another culture.

In summary, learning a foreign language will require that you master the linguistic skills of listening comprehension, speaking, reading, and writing but the mastery of a foreign language will also provide you with the passport to move in and understand other cultures.

$\mathcal{G}$LOSSARY

Here follows a list of words or phrases that appear in the various chapters of the book. The understanding of the meaning of these words will help you in a discussion or explanation of the ways in which your language or the language you are studying functions. (Whenever possible, examples will be cited from the English language.)

Adjective—a content word that is used to modify or describe a noun or pronoun. (Examples in English of adjectives are *big, pretty, delicious, impossible.*)

Adverb—a content word that is used to modify or qualify a verb, adjective, or another adverb. (Examples in English of adverbs are *well, soon, quickly, frequently.* Many adverbs in English are formed by adding the suffix *-ly* to an adjective.)

Body language—the various stances or gestures used to give non-verbal (i.e., unspoken) signals that may or may not accompany speech. (For example, in answer to the question: "Do you care if he comes along?" a shrug, grimace, or shake of the head would serve as a non-verbal answer.

Case—a grammatical concept used to indicate the role a noun or pronoun plays in relation to the verb in a sentence. (In English we have two cases: subject and object. Latin has six.)

Cognates—words in different languages that are similar in form because they are descended from the same word in an ancient language and have more or less the same meaning. (Examples would include English *brother* and German *Bruder*; Spanish *madre* and Italian *madre*, both descended from Latin *mater*.)

Conjunction—a function word that is used to connect other parts of speech as well as phrases and clauses. (Examples of conjunctions in English include: *and, or, but, when, since*.)

Decoding—the process of deriving meaning from what is heard or read that is involved in the passive linguistic skills of listening comprehension and reading.

Determiner—a function word used to mark a noun. (Examples in English include *the, a/an, some, this, my*.)

Distribution—refers to where a sound occurs in relation to other sounds in a syllable or to where a class of words occur in relation to other words in a phrase or sentence.

Encoding—the active process of joining together all the meaningful units and linguistic signals to produce an understandable output.

Fluency—the ability to understand and make oneself understood in a language; competence in the four linguistic skills of listening comprehension, speaking, reading, and writing.

Gender—a grammatical concept used to determine nouns, pronouns (and in some languages, adjectives) as being masculine, feminine or neuter. (In English, *he/him* is masculine, *she/her* is feminine, and *it* is neuter.)

Grammar—the set of rules in a language for forming words, phrases, clauses, and sentences; grammar includes morphology and syntax.

Graphemes—the written symbols of a language. (In English and Greek, for example, the graphemes are the letters of the alphabet.)

Idiomatic expression—a group of two or more words whose collective meaning is not readily deduced from the meanings of its constituent parts. (Examples of idiomatic expressions in English would include: *to catch fire, to beat around the bush, to eat crow.*)

Inflective (language)—a language (such as Latin) in which the stem of a word carries the meaning of the word but never occurs alone; the stem only occurs with an ending that indicates the function of the word. (For example, in Latin the words

puella and **agricola** are subjects

puellam and **agricolam** are objects

so, in the sentences

Puella agricolam videt. "The girl sees the farmer."

Puellam agricola videt. "The farmer sees the girl."

the endings of the nouns indicate whether they are the subject or object of the verb.)

Intransitive (verb)—a verb that does not take a direct object. (Examples in English are: *to arrive, to fall, to die.*)

Inversion—the reversal in order of a verb and its subject to signal a question. (For example, in English the subject (*you*) and the auxiliary verb (*will*) of the statement *You will talk to him* are inverted to form the question: *Will you talk to him?*)

Lexicon—a list of vocabulary items.

Lingua Franca—a common language that speakers of different languages use to communicate among themselves.

Linguistic relativity—the theory proposed by the linguist B. Whorf that speakers of different languages view the world in different ways due to the different ways in which their languages permit or cause them to describe the world.

Linguistics—the study of how languages in general operate, of how their systems and subsystems interrelate.

Minimal pair—two words that differ in pronunciation by a single sound. (For example in English: *bat/cat, bat/bet, bat/bad* are minimal pairs.)

Morpheme—a unit of meaning that combines with other units of meaning to form words. (In English the words *unfit* and *cats* each contain two morphemes.)

Morphology—the subsystem of language that considers the ways in which words are constructed from one or more morphemes.

Noun—a content word used to name a person, place, thing, or idea. (Examples in English include *car, beauty, beach, season.*)

Number—a grammatical concept used to distinguish nouns, pronouns, adjectives, and verbs as being singular or plural. (In English *a dog* is singular, *those chickens* is plural.)

Person—a grammatical concept used to describe a verb's subject as being first ("*I*"), second ("*you*"), or third ("*he/she/it*") person.

Phoneme—a unit of sound, not to be confused with the written letter used to represent the sound. (For example, the English word *coughed* is written with seven letters but contains only four sounds, or phonemes, and in phonemic transcription those four sounds would be rendered as /kôft/.)

Phonology—the system of sounds in any language.

Prefix—a morpheme that occurs before the stem of a word. (For example, in English: the prefixes *im-, re-, un-* all change the meanings of the stems in the following words: *impossible, rewrite, unlikely.*)

Preposition—a function word that is used to introduce a phrase. (Examples of prepositions in English include *to, from, for, with, without.*)

Pronoun—a function word used to replace a noun or noun phrase. Examples in English include *I, we, him, us, them, mine, yours.*)

Romance language—one of the languages descended from the parent language Latin. The Romance languages are French, Spanish, Italian, Portuguese, Rumanian, and Romansch.

Semantics—the subsystem of language that deals with the relationship between words and things or concepts to which the words refer.

Slang—informal words or expressions that are used in place of more "proper" or "correct" language.

Syllable—a breath group consisting of one or more sounds separated from other breath groups by a slight pause. (In English, there is one vowel sound per syllable.)

Syntax—the rules that a language employs to combine words into phrases, clauses, and sentences.

Structure—any linguistic construction in which two or more words are combined into a larger "unit of meaning": phrase, clause, sentence. For example, the sentence:

The young girl ran into the house to look for her mother because she was afraid.

contains

noun phrases: *the young girl, the house, her mother*
adverbial phrase: *into the house*
verb phrase: *to look for her mother*
clause: *because she was afraid*

Suffix—a morpheme that follows the stem of a word. (For example, *-ly, -s, -ed* are suffixes in the following words: *godly, cats, walked.*)

Target language—the language that you are attempting to master.

Tense—a grammatical concept relating to when the action of a verb takes place, e.g., present, past, or future. (In English we would say that the verb in *He runs* is in the *present* tense; in *He ran* it is in the *past* tense; and in *He will run* the verb is in the *future* tense.)

Transitive (verb)—a verb that takes a direct object. The direct object receives the action of the transitive verb. (In the following sentences the verbs are transitive because they perform an action upon the direct object:

We watched the movie.

He didn't finish his homework.)

Verb—a content word that indicates actions or states of being. (Examples of verbs in English include: *to run, to eat, to die, to become, to be.*)

Voice—a grammatical concept that refers to whether the action of the verb is performed by the subject (in which case the verb is in the *active* voice) or whether the action is performed to/on the subject (in which case the verb is in the *passive* voice). In the sentences:

Henry ate the sandwich. (The verb is in the active voice.)

The sandwich was eaten by Henry. (The verb is in the passive voice.)

Word order—the order in which the parts of speech occur in relation to one another in the formation of a phrase, clause, or sentence. (For example, in the English noun phrase *the four broken cups* the order must be Determiner + Numeral + Adjective + Noun.)

$\mathscr{F}$OR FURTHER READING

Bloomfield, Leonard. *Language*. Chicago: University of Chicago Press, 1984.

Bodmer, Frederick. *The Loom of Language*. New York: Norton, 1985.

Brown-Azarowicz, Marjory et al. *Yes! You Can Learn a Foreign Language*. Lincolnwood, Ill.: Passport Books, 1988.

Crystal, David. *The Cambridge Encyclopedia of Language*. New York and Cambridge: Cambridge University Press.

Goldman, Norma, and Ladislas Szymanski. *English Grammar for Students of Latin*. Jacqueline Morton, ed. Ann Arbor, Mich.: Olivia and Hill, 1983.

Farber, Barry. *How to Learn Any Language: Quickly, Easily, Inexpensively, and On Your Own*. New York: Carol Publishing Group, 1991.

Fuller, Graham E. *How to Learn a Foreign Language*. Washington: Storm King Press, 1991.

Hayakawa, S.I., and Alan R. Hayakawa. *Language in Thought and Action*. Fifth ed. San Diego: Harvest Books, 1989.

Marshall, Terry. *Whole World Guide to Language Learning*. Yarmouth, Maine: Intercultural Press, 1990.

Pei, Mario. *The Story of Language*. New York: NAL, 1984.

Pei, Mario. *Voices of Man*. New York: AMS Press, 1991.

Tinkel, A. J. *Explorations in Language*. New York and Cambridge: Cambridge University Press, 1988.

ℐNDEX